THE GENTLE ART OF
VERBAL SELF-DEFENSE WORKBOOK

by Suzette Haden Elgin

Illustrations by Randy Farran

DORSET PRESS
New York

First published in 1987 by Dorset Press, a division of
Marboro Books Corporation

ISBN 0-88029-118-4

Printed in the United States of America
M 9 8 7 6 5 4

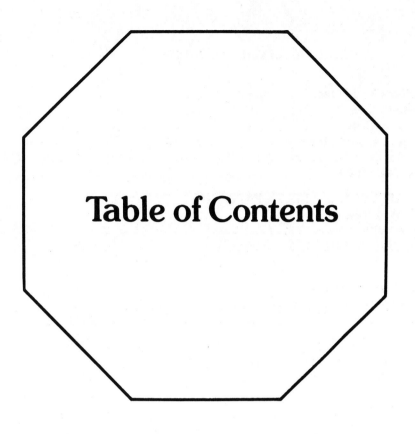

Table of Contents

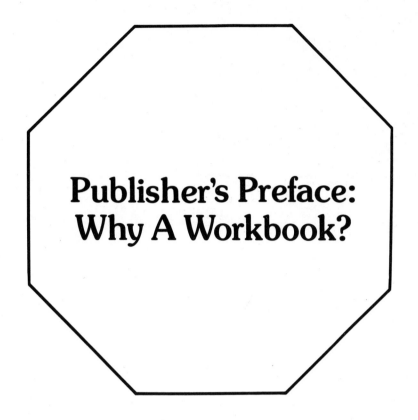

Publisher's Preface: Why A Workbook?

Over 160,000 people now own *The Gentle Art of Verbal Self-Defense*. From the very first printing readers have written requesting a workbook for the revolutionary techniques taught in *The Gentle Art of Verbal Self-Defense*. Responding to this demand, Suzette Haden Elgin has developed the *Gentle Art Workbook* specifically for you to practice and improve the verbal self-defense skills she defined in *The Gentle Art*.

In daily life hostile words can be as psychologically devastating as hostile acts. Dr. Elgin's techniques for identifying and stopping verbal abuse have dramatically changed people's lives—particularly for 'tough contact' professionals such as emergency room physicians, police officers or teachers. As public awareness of the concept of verbal abuse has grown, more and more people are turning to *The Gentle Art of Verbal Self-Defense* for the skills to check the verbal violence they face every day.

Read *The Gentle Art* before you use the *Workbook*. The *Workbook* does not repeat the information in *The Gentle Art*. By practicing verbal self-defense techniques in a series of entertaining exercises specially designed by an expert in the field, you will acquire further skills and experience in identifying, defusing and avoiding verbal abuse.

Further support and information may be obtained by writing to the American Syntonics Association, a non-profit educational and scientific organization concerned with the language environment. Send a *self-addressed, stamped envelope* to: American Syntonics Association, P.O. Box 9182, Tulsa, OK 74157.

How To Use This Workbook

This workbook has been written for use with THE GENTLE ART OF VERBAL SELF-DEFENSE, and is keyed to that book. Its four parts will give you an opportunity for extensive practice with the verbal self-defense techniques presented in THE GENTLE ART. Clear instructions and complete answer pages have been provided for each section.

There are three general items of information that you need before you begin:

(1) You may find the tests for identifying your preferred Satir Modes and Sensory Modes a little long. They're long because tests of that kind with only a few items give you meaningless results. If you don't have time to do them in a single session, just break them up into parts that are convenient for you.

(2) In all the example sentences you will find the same system used for marking stress. Normal stress will be indicated by italics. Abnormal stress (the kind you hear in verbal attacks, for example, or in situations of crisis and confrontation) is indicated by capital letters, as in THE GENTLE ART.

(3) Many of the instructions in this workbook tell you to *write* something. It may be that writing is not the way you like to work. In that case, use a tape recorder instead—either method will serve equally well.

Enjoy the workbook.

Suzette Haden Elgin

PART ONE:
The Satir Modes

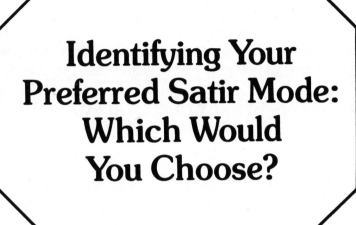

Identifying Your Preferred Satir Mode: Which Would You Choose?

COMPUTER

LEVELER

PLACATER

BLAMER

DISTRACTER

INSTRUCTIONS

Here are ten brief scenarios presenting common situations in everyday life. At the end of each one, you'll find a set of five possible sequences that you might say if you were involved in the situation—one in each of the Satir Modes. For each scenario, decide which of the responses is the one you would prefer. It may be that none of them is what you ordinarily would say; that's all right. Just decide which one, if you had to say one of them, would be your choice. (Resist the temptation to choose the one that you think is the "right" thing to say; imagine yourself in the situation and choose the one that is really most likely for *you*.) Draw a circle around the letter

3

beside your choice. Then, when you've finished the section, write down the number of choices you made from each group in the spaces provided.

SCENARIO ONE

You are a parent, shopping in a large department store with your two small children (ages 8 and 6). Right in the middle of the housewares, the children begin to argue; almost immediately one is crying and the other is screaming. People are looking at you in considerable annoyance. WHAT WOULD YOU SAY?

    a. "If you don't stop that INstantly, you are never going ANYwhere with me again—and I MEAN that!" (BLAMING)

    b. "Children, I know you're tired, and I know this is boring. All the same, cut it out. I MEAN it." (LEVELING)

    c. "Children, I know you're tired, and I'm not mad at you, okay? But I'll tell you what . . . WE can make a DEAL! You stop making all that noise, and I'll take you to get some ice cream just as soon as we're through here, okay?" (PLACATING)

    d. "Listen, you kids are driving me CRAZY, acting like that! You CUT IT out, or ELSE! YOU know how I am; I love you VERY much, and I would NEVer punish you unless there was REALLY a good reason. But there is no excuse for public scenes. I MEAN that!" (DISTRACTING)

    e. "Children who cannot control themselves in public do not go out in public. If that's not clear, an explanation can easily be arranged. This is NOT a joke." (COMPUTING)

SCENARIO TWO

Your boss has called you in and accused you of stealing five dollars from petty cash. You did take it, but it was an oversight—you took the money on a day when you'd forgotten your wallet, and you meant to put it back the following morning—you just forgot. You don't want to lose your job. WHAT WOULD YOU SAY?

    a. "You have NO RIGHT to accuse me of that. I have NEVER stolen anything in my enTIRE LIFE! HOW COULD YOU SAY a thing like that to me?" (B)

    b. "You KNOW I wouldn't steal—I'm NOT that kind of PERson! Oh, what did I ever DO to make you suspect me of a thing like that?" (P)

    c. "Taking five dollars from petty cash is not STEALing. There are very few people who have never borrowed a few dollars and then forgotten to return it. The money will be replaced immediately." (C)

    d. "ME? STEAL from petty CASH? WHY do you always jump to conclusions about me like that? It is quite clear that there has been a misunderstanding." (D)

e. "I should not have done that, and I CERtainly should not have forgotten about it. It won't happen again." (L)

SCENARIO THREE

You're in your doctor's examining room, and you have already had to wait quite a while. You hear a tap at the door and think, "AT LAST!" But it's not the doctor, it's the nurse, who says, "It'll only be a few minutes longer now! I *know* you don't mind, but I thought I'd just let you know. WHAT WOULD YOU SAY?

a. "I do mind. I'll wait—but I DO MIND." (L)
b. "Oh, thanks! Of COURSE I don't mind—I *know* how BUSY doctors are!" (P)
c. "Will YOU please explain to me why *I* am ALWAYS the one that gets PICKED to WAIT?" (B)
d. "Taking it for granted that a patient is willing to put up with interminable waiting is not necessarily a good idea, Nurse." (C)
e. "Just a little while? That's what you ALWAYS say, you know! There's no excuse for this sort of disorganization. But I'll wait, sure . . . I didn't have anything special to do this morning anyway." (D)

SCENARIO FOUR

It's your first day in a math class, and the instructor is new to you, too. You hear the word "lambda" and you don't know what it means; you're afraid you won't understand the rest of the lecture if you don't find out. But everybody else DOES seem to understand. WHAT WOULD YOU SAY?

a. "I know this is probably a stupid QUEStion; but WHAT's a lambda?" (P)
b. "If you don't explain the TERMS you use, nobody IN here is going to LEARN anything! What's a LAMBda?" (B)
c. "Lambda. No doubt that's a familiar term, but a definition would be helpful." (C)
d. "What's a lambda? I ought to know, but I don't. I don't understand why there is always SOMEthing in the VERY FIRST LECTURE that I've NEVer HEARD of before! Statistically, that is surely not probable. Is it?" (D)
e. "I have no idea what lambda means. Would you define it for me, please?" (L)

SCENARIO FIVE

You're sure the person at the cash register has given you a counterfeit five dollar bill in your change, but your suggestion that this has happened is hotly denied. There are a lot of people waiting in line behind you. WHAT WOULD YOU SAY?

a. "Oh, well . . . it's ONly five DOLlars! I'm probably mistaken." (P)

b. "What's the MATTER with you? Do you enJOY keeping all these people waiting in LINE? Not that I don't KNOW how it feels to make a mistake—I DO! And I know this is very inconVENient for you, when you're so BUSy! But principles are principles. Don't you think so?" (D)

c. "Maybe I'm wrong, but I don't think so. I'll wait while you get the manager." (L)

d. "If YOU think you're going to get away with THIS, you are VERY mistaken! NObody cheats ME! You call the manager, and we'll just SEE who's right!" (B)

e. "Situations of this kind do arise from time to time; everyone is aware of that. However, the manager should be called." (C)

SCENARIO SIX

You're late for your mother's sixtieth birthday dinner, and you don't have a good excuse. You just plain forgot, and now the whole family is staring at you, waiting for your explanation. WHAT WOULD YOU SAY?

a. "I am such an IDiot! Can you believe it . . . I was so BUSY this morning! You're not mad at me, are you? You know how I am . . . brain like a steel sieve! Happy birthday, Mother!" (P)

b. "I'm sorry I'm late—please forgive me. Happy birthday, Mother." (L)

c. "Lateness is rude, and very rarely excusable. Apologies are certainly in order. Happy birthday, Mother." (C)

d. "I'm late, I know . . . I'm SO sorry! Anybody who would do something like this . . . WHY does this kind of thing always happen to ME? Happy birthday, Mother." (D)

e. "If you people hadn't insisted on having this dinner right in the middle of the busiest part of my working day, I wouldn't have BEEN late! Happy birthday, Mother." (B)

SCENARIO SEVEN

You have an elderly aunt that you're very fond of, and you're taking her out to dinner at your local country club; you know you'll run into business associates and customers there. When Aunt Elizabeth comes downstairs, all ready to leave with you, she is beautifully dressed—but she is wearing her bedroom slippers. WHAT WOULD YOU SAY?

a. "Aunt Elizabeth, you've forgotten to take off your bedroom slippers." (L)

b. "Aunt Elizabeth, you KNOW I would never criticize you, and I think you look LOVEly no matter WHAT you wear . . . but are you SURE you want to go out in your bedroom slippers?" (P)

c. "Aunt Elizabeth, for crying out loud! WHY have you still got your bedroom slippers on?" (B)

d. "Aunt Elizabeth . . . darling . . . I mean, only SNOBS worry about what others are wearing. But do you REALLY think bedroom slippers are the right thing to wear to the COUNTRY CLUB? Not that I CARE, you understand. The privileges of age, right?" (D)

e. "When someone dresses in a hurry, it's easy for them to overlook small details. Changing shoes, for example." (C)

SCENARIO EIGHT

Your spouse is determined to go back to school and finish a degree. You are opposed to that, and you feel that it's a waste of money. You say so, and are told that you're just objecting because you don't have a degree yourself and you're jealous. That happens to be true, but you are absolutely determined not to admit it. WHAT WOULD YOU SAY?

a. "I don't want to talk about it any longer." (L)

b. "That's a STUPid thing to say! DON'T BE RIDICulous!" (B)

c. "Those who are unsure of their own motives very often try to hide that by making accusations about the motives of other people." (C)

d. "ME? Come on. I've NEVER wanted a degree! People who need degrees to be sure of their own worth are just insecure. But you do whatever you want to—*I* certainly don't care!" (D)

e. "Oh, that's not TRUE! That's silly. But I'm sorry I sounded that way—I didn't MEAN to." (P)

SCENARIO NINE

You are feeling dizzy and weak and sick. You tell the friends you're out with about it and say you'd like to go home. The response you get is, "Don't be silly, you'll forget about it and feel a LOT better if you go on with us!" WHAT WOULD YOU SAY?

a. "If you really CARED about how I felt, you'd take me HOME!" (B)

b. "You're probably right—I'm sorry to be such a pain in the neck." (P)

c. "That's easily said. But sick people are better off at home in their beds." (C)

d. "Oh, sure . . . you're right. I'm always imagining things. But dizziness is genuinely unpleasant; people who are dizzy may black out and spoil the whole evening. Why don't you think about how *I* feel about this?" (D)

e. "If you don't want to take me home, I'll take a cab." (L)

SCENARIO TEN

Some close friends have brought their brand new baby over to show you. You think it is a *very* ugly baby. Your friends ask you what you think of their child. WHAT WOULD YOU SAY?

a. "What do *I* know about babies? No one who doesn't HAVE a child is any judge of babies, that's well known. I'm sure it's a TERRIFIC baby!" (D)

b. "YOU know I don't know anything about babies! Why are you asking ME?" (B)

c. "I think it's a terRIFFIC BABY! But *you* know me, I don't even HAVE a baby, what do *I* know? Don't YOU think it's a terrific baby? YOU'RE the EXperts!" (P)

d. "That's an interesting baby. No question about it!" (L)

Now, count up your choices and enter the totals here:

BLAMER __1__   COMPUTER __C__   PLACATER __4__   DISTRACTER __8__

LEVELER __1__

Six or more in any one category indicates a clear preference for that Mode; a score of three or less indicates a clear NON-preference. A set like BLAMER (5), COMPUTER (5), indicates a mixed preference. However, because you aren't really *feeling* the stress described in the scenarios, it's harder to determine your preferred Satir Mode with a written test than it is for the Sensory Modes. If the results you get are confusing, the activities below may help clarify them.

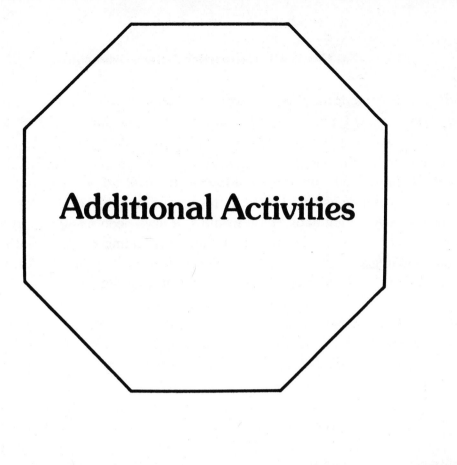

Additional Activities

COMPUTER

LEVELER

PLACATER

BLAMER

DISTRACTER

• Try to pay close attention to the language that you use in stressful situations and confrontations for a while—not to remember the exact words you use, but to become aware of which Satir Mode you tend to fall back on. Make a note of your choices under stress until you see a pattern. This isn't easy, because when you are under stress you'll have trouble remembering that you want to pay attention to this task. But if you keep trying, after a while you'll begin to be more aware of your language behavior and it won't be so hard to do. If you like, get someone else to help you in this project; maybe your spouse or a close friend would be willing to observe and then tell you later, "I think you were using Blamer Mode that time." You may find that the pattern is tied to the ROLE you are filling; for example, you may notice that in a confrontation with your spouse you seem to prefer Blamer

Mode, but in a confrontation with your doctor you are more likely to Placate, or vice versa. This is typical. It is very unusual for a person who is under stress to choose one and only one Satir Mode no matter what the situation.

- Pay attention to the language behavior of *other* people in stressful situations, especially those in which you are not personally involved. Ask yourself, "Is that the language I would be using if I were in the same situation?" If not, decide what you *would* have said. What Satir Mode would you have been using? A strong negative reaction to someone else's language behavior, a feeling of "Oh, that's all wrong! He/she *should* be saying . . . " is a good indication that you would have used a different Satir Mode, and is a clue to your own preferences.

- Try some role-playing with a friend. Deliberately try setting up some confrontations between the two of you, just for practice. There's no real stress in such situations [IF THERE IS, STOP—YOU HAVE A REAL CONFRONTATION INSTEAD OF AN EXERCISE!]; but the choices you make among the Modes in such role-playing give you additional information about your preferences.

- Try deliberately *violating* your preference. Make a rule for yourself that for one whole day, in all situations of stress, you will use only Computer Mode. (Obviously you don't do this in an emergency, or when real harm could result. Just in garden variety confrontations.) If you find this easy to do, it's a clue that Computer Mode is your *natural* preference; if not, it's probably awkward for you. Try the same experiment with the other Modes until you find the one you're most comfortable with.

- When you're watching television or movies and you see language confrontations, notice which Satir Modes the participants are using. Ask yourself, "In that situation, would I be using that Mode or some other one?"

Identifying
The Satir Modes:
Which One
Is Being Used?

INSTRUCTIONS

The skit below presents a situation of severe stress. Read it all the way through once, to get a feeling for the whole sequence. Then go back and read it again. This time, stop at the end of each line of dialogue and fill in the blank with the name of the Satir Mode you believe the speaker is using. To check your work, go to the answer section at the end of the chapter.

SKIT

The scene is a family dinner, celebrating the Fourth of July. It's very hot in the room, and nobody is comfortable. Here are the speakers at the table:

ANN (the grandmother)

MARY, Ann's daughter, and husband BILL

BOB, Ann's unmarried adult son

JUDITH, Ann's daughter, and husband GEORGE

JENNIFER, Mary and Bill's six-year-old-daughter

1. MARY: "Jennifer, WHY are you just sitting there playing with your food? Do you realize how long your grandmother stood in the kitchen in this horrible heat to COOK THAT FOOD?"

Blaming   _B or D_

_____

2. ANN: "THERE YOU go! Will you PLEASE tell me why it is that EVERY time you bring Jennifer here to SEE me you spend the WHOLE VISIT PICKING ON HER?"

_B_

_____
Blaming

3. MARY: "PICKING on her! *Really*, Mother! HOW do you expect me to teach the child any manners if you ALways step in and take her side AGAINST me?"

_D_

_____
Blaming

4. BILL: "Mary, you KNOW I would never try to interfere in a discussion between you and your mother—"

_P_

_____

5. JENNIFER: "I'm not playing with my food. I'm not hungry. THAT's why I'm not eating."

_L_

_____

6. JUDITH: "Well, you know how I am, I believe people should at least TRY to get along with their own family, and I do NOT believe anybody should tell other people how to raise their children, even if the child DOES interrupt her father right in the middle of a sentence! How would I know? I don't even HAVE a child. But don't all of you think it would be nicer if—"

Placating   _D_

_____

7. GEORGE: "It is INCREDIBLE how women are able to turn any conversation, no matter what its subject, into an argument about whether to have children or not!"

_____ B____ C_____

_____

8. BOB: "This is ridiculous, folks. Let's start all over."

_____ C____ L_____

_____

9. JUDITH: "Now my OWN BROTHer is attacking me! I guess I must have really put my FOOT in my mouth . . . I'M sorry, everybody! I don't know WHAT I was THINKing about! None of this is any of MY business! Mother, this is such a lovely dinner; I'd give anything if I could fry chicken the way you do, but I'm such a ninny, I can't do anything right . . . Here, Jenny, let Aunt Judith cut that up for you, dear."

_____ P____ D_____

10. MARY: "You're wasting your time. She won't eat it."

_____ B____ L_____

11. BOB: "I wouldn't eat either, if people kept tormenting me like that."

_____ C____ L_____

12. GEORGE: "There is a clear and obvious difference between tormenting a child and DISCIplining a child."

_____ C_____

13. ANN: "Oh, PLEASE stop! NONE of you have any manners! Oh, I don't really mean that . . . of _course_ you have manners . . . but it seems to me that no matter HOW hard I try, no matter WHAT I do to try to make things nice, you NEVER appreciate it! The way some people lose their entire minds if the temperature goes above ninety degrees is almost impossible to understand. Oh, you've spoiled the WHOLE DAY! What did I DO to bring on all of this?"

_____ B____ D_____

_____

14. BILL: "Well, Mary, I HOPE YOU'RE SATisfied. You've managed to ruin the holiday for every single person here, the way you ALways do. ConGRATulations, honey— you've destroyed another family dinner!"

_____

_____

Additional Activities

- Choose a book or story with long stretches of dialogue presenting language interactions that involve stress and confrontation. Take sections of these interactions and work with them just as you did with the skit above, deciding which Satir Mode is being used for each speech.

- Do the same thing for several television shows. Try a situation comedy that has reasonably realistic plots, a talk show, and a soap opera. Keep track, roughly, of the Satir Modes being used.

  If you have a videocassette recorder and can use it to tape some examples of each type of show for further analysis, try answering the following questions:

  a. Are there any patterns that seem to go with the type of show? Do the people on the soap opera seem to do more Leveling than those on the other shows, or vice

15

versa? On the talk show, do the people use the Satir Modes that you would expect them to use if they weren't on television?

b. Do you notice interesting patterns in the way one Satir Mode or another is assigned to men or to women on different types of shows? What about the way particular Modes are assigned to elderly characters, as opposed to very young ones? How about ethnic groups' lines—do you see a pattern in which all Lackawhackians are always portrayed as doing nothing but Blaming?

c. When you've had some practice doing this sort of activity, start considering how *believable* the language choices are. Would real people make the Satir Mode choices that the characters and talk show participants make? Would you?

d. See if you can clearly identify the preferred Satir Modes of some of your family, friends, associates, and colleagues. Do you notice anyone who really does seem always to choose a single Mode, no matter what the situation? Do you see clear preferences for particular Modes in certain types of stressful situations, regardless of the person involved? When you've made quite a few of these identifications, look them over carefully—do you see any differences that you feel are clearly due to sexual gender?

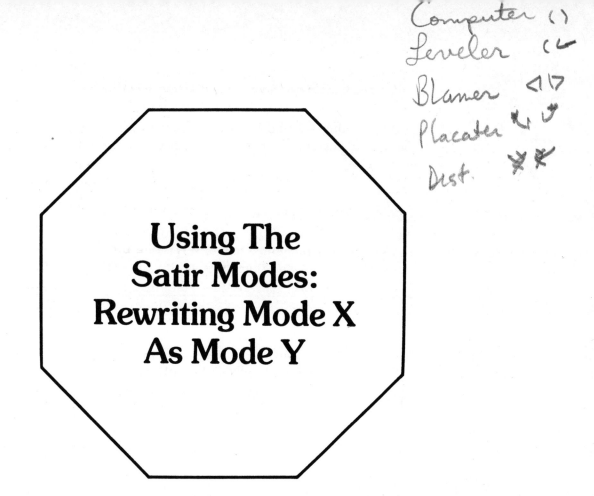

Using The Satir Modes: Rewriting Mode X As Mode Y

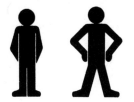 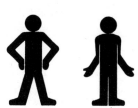  

INSTRUCTIONS

Here are ten brief exchanges written to demonstrate the use of a particular Satir Mode. At the end of the second speaker's line you'll see a letter identifying the Mode used and telling you to rewrite that sequence in a *different* Mode. Try to express approximately the same meaning, but don't worry if you can't get an exact match. There are suggested answers at the end of the chapter; there are no "right" answers, of course.

1. X: "What do you think—should I buy that chair or not?"
   Y: "People should make up their own minds about their own furniture."
   (C, rewrite as B)

   why don't you make up your own mind?
   You never do!

2. X: "You NEVER say anything nice to me! WHY IS that?"
   Y: "Because YOU never say anything nice to ME, THAT'S why!" (B, rewrite as P)

   Oh I'm sorry I know!

3. X: "I'm so tired . . . I just don't think I can go to that meeting tonight."
   Y: "Don't be silly, YOU'RE not tired! Oh, MAYBE you're tired, I could be wrong. But one game of tennis is not tiring to a normal person." (D, rewrite as L)

   So don't go

4. X: "She doesn't seem to like me very much . . . what do you suppose is wrong?"
   Y: "You ALways think nobody likes you! You're PARanoid, you _know that_?" (B, rewrite as D)

   Oh maybe your right shucks I dont
   know does she?

5. X: "I can't DO this puzzle—it's too _hard_. How about helping me with it?"
   Y: "No one who has any purpose in life wastes time doing puzzles." (C, rewrite as B)

   You are stupid etc

6. X: "_Careful_! You're going to trip over that chair!"
   Y: "I am forEVer doing that! I swear, I am the CLUMsiest person . . . I don't know why you ever go _any_where with me!" (P, rewrite as C)

7. X: "Are you mad at me about something?"
   Y: "Yes I am. I'm _furious_ with you." (L, rewrite as P)

8. X: "I hear her kids are ALways in trouble with the police. Isn't that awful?"
   Y: "Oh, YOU know me, I don't like to criticize other people! Shoot, I'm not perfect either, AM I?" (P, rewrite as L)

   _____

   _____

9. X: "I am FOURTEEN YEARS OLD. I don't HAVE to be home by ten o'clock anymore!"
   Y: "You are fourteen years old. You are correct about that. Period." (L, rewrite as B)

   _____

   _____

10. X: "Would you mind picking up the kids this afternoon? I've got so much to do, I don't see how I can possibly do it."
    Y: "Did it ever occur to you that OTHER people might ALSO HAVE THINGS TO DO?" (B, rewrite as P)

    _____

    _____

Additional Activities

- Rewrite each of the short interactions above in some *other* Satir Modes. (There's probably very little point in practicing Distracter Mode rewrites, unless you suspect that it's the one you prefer—in that case, Distracter rewrites will help you identify the kind of responses you should try to eliminate from your language behavior.) If you find any one of the Modes especially easy—or especially hard—to use this way, that's additional information about your own Satir Mode preferences.

- Play a game with the Satir Modes. Use a spinner, or a set of labeled cards. The first player has to say something in the Mode he/she gets on the spin or the draw; the next player must do the same, but what is said has to be a possible response to what the *first* player said, and so on through the game. Any player who can't think of a response in the Mode he/she gets has to drop out, and the last person in the game wins. (NOTE: For a simpler version of the game, limit the "conversation" to only three turns, or only five turns, after which the next player is allowed to start a new sequence. The higher the number of turns is set, the harder the game will be.)

- Rewrite a familiar folktale so that every line of dialogue in it is in a particular Satir Mode. For example, do "The Three Bears" or "The Little Red Hen" with every speech rewritten in Blamer Mode. (And if you can get a few friends to act out these revised stories with you, by all means do so. Pay close attention to the results you get. Try a Blamer version of one, and then a Placater version of the same story, and act out both versions.)

- If you have television access to Congressional debate, and a VCR, record half an hour or so of debate in which at least three members participate and things aren't dull. Play your tape a few times to become familiar with it. Now, rewrite some of the utterances in different Satir Modes and consider what the results might have been if the speakers had done that.

- Watch some television shows with the sound *off*. Do you think you can tell which Satir Mode is being used, from the body language alone? Try the same activity with the sound so low that you can't understand the words, but you can hear the intonation—can you identify the Modes?

- If you have a videotape with lots of dialogue that you can watch a number of times, you can do a very interesting experiment. Watch just a few lines at a time, with the sound off and then with it on. Watch for conflicts—dialogue where the speaker's body language doesn't match the words used, or vice versa. Can you tell whether the actor is doing this on purpose, to create an effect, or is unaware of the mismatch? With *good* actors, it should never be an accident. (You might also try recording a few political speeches and giving them the same kind of analysis; the results can be amazing.)

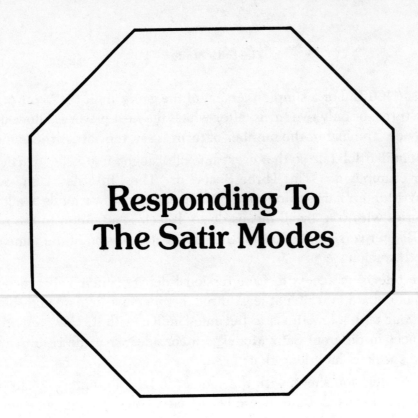

Responding To
The Satir Modes

INSTRUCTIONS

Here are ten brief interactions using the Satir Modes. In each one, two lines are filled in and another is left blank for *you* to fill in. Write in the line, following the rules for responding to Satir Modes. Remember that whether you match a Satir Mode or not depends on the situation—it will *always* escalate that Mode, so that Blaming at someone who is Blaming causes more Blaming, Leveling at someone who is Leveling causes more Leveling, and so on. And when you don't know *what* to do, Computer Mode is always safest. You'll find suggested answers at the end of the chapter.

The Satir Modes

INTERACTION ONE

SPOUSE X: "I'm really worried about Tracy's grades."

SPOUSE Y: "Did you notice they were predicting storms for today?"

SPOUSE X: "_____

_____"

INTERACTION TWO

PATIENT: "Doctor, I have a terrible pain in my stomach."

DOCTOR: "You ALWAYS think you have stomach pain, and it's always your imagination. Personally, I think you get a pain in your stomach when you don't want to *do* something."

PATIENT: "_____

_____"

INTERACTION THREE

SUPERVISOR: "Your work is unsatisfactory—we can't go on like this."

EMPLOYEE: "That's not FAIR! Anytime something goes wrong around here, you jump on ME, no matter WHOSE fault it is!"

SUPERVISOR: "_____

_____"

INTERACTION FOUR

FRIEND X: "You know something . . . it's dangerous to smoke as much as you do."

FRIEND Y: "PLEASE don't say that to me! You only say that to HURT me—you KNOW I'm going to quit as soon as things are a little better at work . . . DON'T say stuff that makes me feel rotten!"

FRIEND X: "_____

_____"

INTERACTION FIVE

WAITRESS: "Look, I don't make substitutions. You don't like that, you can go eat someplace else."

CUSTOMER: "WOW, do you have rotten manners! How do you keep your customers?"

WAITRESS: "_____

_____"

23

INTERACTION SIX

> *FRIEND X:* "I can't stand this traffic. It's DRIVING ME CRAZY! I'm not kidding. WHY am I always the one that has to stay late and then gets stuck in the rush hour this way? There is surely an explanation. I think."
>
> *FRIEND Y:* "I know . . . I can't stand it EITHer. LOOK at that! We're going to be here for HOURS! We'll miss the plane. You ALways make me miss-planes—this is the third *time.* Maybe it's my fault, though; I'm sorry I snapped at you."
>
> *FRIEND X:* "_____
> _____"

INTERACTION SEVEN

> *CHILD (to another child):* "You GIVE me that! YOU CAN'T PLAY with my stuff!"
>
> *PARENT:* "HOW COME you're always so selfish? Don't you ever think about the way you sound? Don't you even CARE if nobody likes you?"
>
> *CHILD:* "_____
> _____"

INTERACTION EIGHT

> *SPOUSE X:* "Honey . . . please don't ask me to do this. I HATE lying to your mother."
>
> *SPOUSE Y:* "If you REALLY loved me, you wouldn't *act* like that—you'd be GLAD there was something you could do to help me out."
>
> *SPOUSE X:* "_____
> _____"

INTERACTION NINE

> *SALESMAN:* "Look . . . *you* won't be happy with that model. Sure, it's cheaper. But do you REALLY want to risk the lives of your family with a tacky little gadget like that?"
>
> *CUSTOMER:* "How about your tacky little sales spiel?"
>
> *SALESMAN:* "_____
> _____"

INTERACTION TEN

BUS DRIVER: "Please sit down, so I can start the bus."
PASSENGER: "Why? You just get out of remedial driving class?"

BUS DRIVER: "_____

_____"

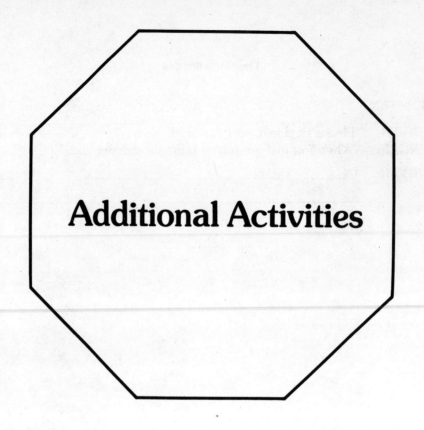

Additional Activities

- For a complete workout in the Satir Modes, try rewriting all of the interactions above, substituting different Modes in many combinations.

- Watch some television shows; listen to some radio call-in shows. Your goal is to spot examples of the following situations:
  a. The Satir Modes are matched, and it works.
  b. The Satir Modes are not matched, and it works.
  c. The Satir Modes are matched, and it fails.
  d. The Satir Modes are not matched, and it fails.

Watch for examples of Computer Mode; can you tell when it's being used because of the emergency fallback rule, and when it's being used for other reasons? (When you become skilled at this, start analyzing the strategy of the speakers. Ask yourself,

"Why was that Satir Mode used that time? What was the speaker trying to do? What would I have done in the same situation?")

- Carry out the same kind of observation for real-world language interactions. Watch closely for different patterns that turn up in crises.

- Try using a new rule: ALWAYS match the Satir Mode coming at you, NO MATTER WHAT. (Don't do this when it would get you into real-world difficulties, obviously. If you feel insecure about it, get some friends to help you do it as a role-playing exercise instead of doing it in spontaneous language interactions.) Pay close attention to what happens. What happens if you flip the rule and NEVER match the Mode?

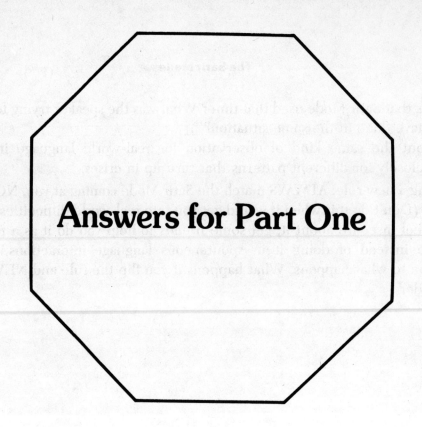

Answers for Part One

A. IDENTIFYING THE SATIR MODES: WHICH ONE IS BEING USED?

1. MARY: Blaming
2. ANN: Blaming
3. MARY: Blaming
4. BILL: Placating
5. JENNIFER: Leveling
6. JUDITH: Placating
7. GEORGE: Computing
8. BOB: Leveling
9. JUDITH: Distracting
10. MARY: Leveling
11. BILL: Leveling

12. GEORGE: Computing
13. ANN: Distracting
14. BILL: Blaming

B. USING THE SATIR MODES: REWRITE MODE X AS MODE Y

1. "Why don't you make up your OWN mind, instead of bothering ME?"
2. "Because YOU aren't nice to ME, you know what I mean? I would NEVER be horrible to ANYbody unless they were horrible to me first, you KNOW that. But maybe I *deserve* to be treated like this . . . I'm *sorry*; I really am."
3. If a game of tennis makes you so tired you don't have enough energy for a meeting, that's not good."
4. "You don't think she likes you? Are you SURE? Some people's behavior is hard to figure out. You're ALways jumping to conclusions—you should WATCH that. But you could be right. I never know whether anybody likes ME or not."
5. "How can you bother me with something so STUPid? Maybe YOU think I don't have anything worthWHILE to do with my time!"
6. "Clumsiness is such a common problem; no doubt it's a nuisance for everybody concerned."
7. "Now, WHY would you think THAT? YOU know how I am! I'LL put up with almost ANYthing!"
8. "I have too many faults of my own to feel comfortable criticizing anybody else. Sorry."
9. "Just because you're fourteen, you think you're the BOSS all of a sudden! Well, let me tell YOU, you are VERY VERY wrong—and you'll remember that or you'll NEVER get to stay out past ten o'clock!"
10. "Sure, I'LL do it. Heck, anything *I* have to do I can ALways put off till LATer!"

C. RESPONDING TO THE SATIR MODES

1. "You have ignored what I said, and you've changed the subject. Let's talk about Tracy's grades." (L,C,L)
2. "Right now, the one thing I don't want to do is pay YOU." (L,L,L)
3. "All right, maybe that's so. Let's talk about it." (L,B,L)
4. "Maybe if I make you feel rotten ENOUGH, you'll stop smoking." (L,P,L)
5. "Maybe people who get too tired say things they shouldn't sometimes." (L,L,C)
6. "This is REALLY awful—I'm getting sick, you know? How could I have been so STUPid, trying to take a plane at five o'clock in the afternoon? But YOU said we HAD to, and you KNOW I always try to go along with people, if I CAN. But I'm going to be *sick*." (D,D,D . . . see what happens?)
7. "No, I don't. You don't care if nobody likes YOU!" (B,B,L)
8. "Of *course* I love you. I love you very much." (L,B,L)
9. "Okay. You got me. There's nothing wrong with the cheap one." (B,L,L)
10. "The safety laws require that all passengers be sitting down before the bus is allowed to start." (L,B,C)

PART TWO:
The Sensory Modes

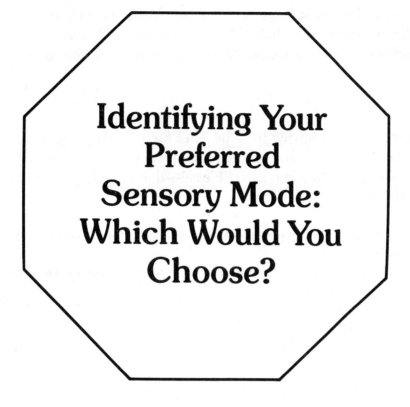

Identifying Your Preferred Sensory Mode: Which Would You Choose?

TOUCH

SIGHT

HEARING

INSTRUCTIONS

Here are fifteen brief scenarios describing common situations in everyday life. At the end of each one you'll find a set of four possible sequences that you might say if you were involved in the situation—one in Sight Mode, one in Hearing Mode, one in Touch Mode, and one that does not use any of the Sensory Modes. For each scenario, decide which of the set of possible sequences you would prefer to say. (It may be that none of them is something you would ordinarily say; that's all right. Just decide which one, if you had to say *one* of them, would be your choice.) Draw a circle around the letter beside your choice. Then, when you've finished the section, write down the number of choices you made from each group in the spaces provided.

SCENARIO ONE

You're in a grocery store, buying fresh peaches for a family party. You're picking up peaches, looking at them, and putting them back down. A middle-aged store employee comes over to you and says, "Please—don't handle the produce!" WHAT WOULD YOU SAY?

    a. "Look, I'm going to buy five pounds of these peaches. But I have to see which ones are *ripe*! (SIGHT)

    b. "Listen, I'm going to buy five pounds of these peaches. But I have to find out which ones are *ripe*!" (HEARING)

    c. "Hey, I came in here to get five pounds of these peaches. But I can't feel which ones are *ripe* without touching them!" (TOUCH)

    d. "Hey, I'm going to buy five pounds of these peaches. But I have to know which ones are *ripe*!" (OTHER)

SCENARIO TWO

You're at your doctor's office for a regular visit about a chronic blood pressure problem. The visit is almost over when you remember that lately you've had an annoying ache in your left ear. You ask your doctor about it, only to be told, "I'm sorry, but you'll have to make another appointment. I don't have time to look at that this morning." WHAT WOULD YOU SAY?

    a. "I see. In that case, I don't have time to write you a check." (S)

    b. "I hear you. In that case, I don't have time to write you a check." (H)

    c. "I get the message. In that case, I don't have time to write you a check." (T)

    d. "I understand. In that case, I don't have time to write you a check." (O)

SCENARIO THREE

Your ten-year-old son has just taken a bath, and has left the bathroom looking like a disaster area. Water on the floor, towels wadded up in the puddles, dirt in the tub . . . the works. WHAT WOULD YOU SAY TO HIM?

a. "It doesn't look to me like any one person could *possibly* make that much mess without help!" (S)

b. "I've never *heard* of any one person being able to make that much mess without help!" (H)

c. I absolutely cannot grasp how any one person could *possibly* make that much mess without help!" (T)

d. "I really do not understand how any one person could *possibly* make that much mess without help!" (O)

SCENARIO FOUR

Your boss has just outlined a plan for new shifts at work and new schedules that baffle you—it sounds ridiculous. You're asked to express your frank opinion. WHAT WOULD YOU SAY?

a. "The only thing that's clear to *me* is that it would never work." (S)

b. "It just sounds to *me* like something that would never work." (H)

c. "All *I* get from it is the feeling that it would never work." (T)

d. "The only thing *I* understand is that it would never work."(O)

SCENARIO FIVE

A friend has just told you a shocking story about your local police chief. You think it must be completely wrong—you don't believe the official would have done such a thing. WHAT WOULD YOU SAY?

a. "The way I look at it, that's got to be either a vicious lie or a ridiculous mistake." (S)

b. "It sounds to me like that's got to be either a vicious lie or a ridiculous mistake. (H)

c. "The way I feel, that's got to be either a vicious lie or a ridiculous mistake." (T)

d. "In my opinion, that's got to be either a vicious lie or a ridiculous mistake." (O)

SCENARIO SIX

Your spouse has just informed you that your joint bank account is $100.00 overdrawn. This comes as a shock to you, because you were sure you had a respectable balance, and you're baffled. WHAT WOULD YOU SAY?

a. "Look, I can't see any way that could have happened." (S)

b. "Listen, I hear you, but there's no way that could have happened."(H)

c. "Hey, I don't get it—there's no way that could have happened." (T)

d. "Wait a minute, I don't believe there's any way that could have happened." (O)

SCENARIO SEVEN

Your child has announced to you that the *only* thing she wants for her birthday is a pony. You know she can't have a pony, but you hate to just say a flat no—you'd like some support from other family members. WHAT WOULD YOU SAY?

a. "A pony, huh? Let's go see what your grandmother would think of that." (S)

b. "A pony, huh? Let's find out how that sounds to your grandmother." (H)

c. "A pony, huh? Let's go find out how your grandmother feels about that." (T)

d. "A pony, huh? You know, I'd like to have your grandmother's opinion on that." (O)

SCENARIO EIGHT

Your boss has just told you a rumor that's going around the office about another employee, and wants to know if you think the story could be true. You *know* it's true, but you'd rather not say so; still, you don't want to actually lie. WHAT WOULD YOU SAY?

a. "I guess I could picture him doing something like that. Maybe." (S)

b. "I guess that sounds like something he might do. Maybe." (H)

c. "I feel like he just might do something like that. Maybe." (T)

d. "I suppose it's possible that he'd do something like that. Maybe." (O)

SCENARIO NINE

All afternoon you've had a strange feeling that the meeting you're in is headed in the wrong direction and getting more muddled by the minute. You feel that you have to say something, but you don't want to be unpleasant about it. WHAT WOULD YOU SAY?

a. "You know, it's not exactly crystal clear to me, but I'm *sure* we're overlooking something important." (S)

b. "You know, there's nothing that exactly rings a bell with me, but I'm *sure* there's something important that's not getting said." (H)

    c. "You know, I can't exactly put my finger on it, but I *really* feel like something important is getting neglected." (T)

    d. "You know, I'm not able to be exactly specific about this, but I'm *sure* we're forgetting something important." (O)

SCENARIO TEN

You have really *goofed*. And now you're having to try to explain your mistake to a group of very angry people, all of whom outrank you. WHAT WOULD YOU SAY?

    a. "Looking back on my decision now, I can see that it was a serious mistake—you're right." (S)

    b. "When I hear my decision discussed now, it sounds like a serious mistake—you're right." (H)

    c. "The feeling I get now is that I really put my foot in it when I made that decision—you're right." (T)

    d. "Thinking about my decision now, I know that it was a serious error—you're right. (O)

SCENARIO ELEVEN

You've just won a very large prize in a lottery, and you're prepared to spend a little money. One of your close friends asks you what you plan to do first. WHAT WOULD YOU SAY?

    a. "Well, I have my eye on a nice little house at the beach." (S)

    b. "Well, a nice little house at the beach would be music to my ears." (H)

    c. "Well, I'd like to get my hands on a nice little house at the beach." (T)

    d. "Well, what I have in mind is a nice little house at the beach." (O)

SCENARIO TWELVE

A friend has just told you that he plans to lose 30 pounds in two weeks by eating only hardboiled eggs, tomatoes, and grapefruit. You disapprove of this, and you don't mind telling him so. WHAT WOULD YOU SAY?

    a. "I take a *very* dim view of crash diets like that!" (S)

    b. "Crash diets like that sound really *crazy* to me!" (H)

    c. "The impression I get of crash diets like that is *very* bad!" (T)

    d. "I have a *very* poor opinion of crash diets like that!" (O)

SCENARIO THIRTEEN

You've just finished working out a plan that is important to you, and you've written it down. Now you want to get some feedback from other people before you do anything more with it, and you take it to one of your friends. WHAT WOULD YOU SAY?

a. "Would you glance over this and tell me if it looks okay to you?" (S)
b. "Would you give this some attention and tell me if it sounds okay to you?" (H)
c. "Would you go over this and let me know if it feels okay to you?" (T)
d. "Would you think about this awhile and let me know if it seems okay to you?" (O)

SCENARIO FOURTEEN

Your younger sister is a nice person, but she has a tendency to go overboard about things and then be sorry later. When she walks into your living room and says "You'll never guess the wonderful idea I've got now!" you know it's happening again, and you wish you could ward it off. WHAT WOULD YOU SAY?

a. "Okay—what are you all starry-eyed about *this* time?" (S)
b. "Okay—what kind of heavenly music are you hearing *this* time?" (H)
c. "Okay—what's got you in its clutches *this* time?" (T)
d. "Okay—what's causing all the excitement in your head *this* time?" (O)

SCENARIO FIFTEEN

You've just told everybody in your group what you plan to do over the holiday weekend, and you expected some kind of reaction. But they're all just sitting there, saying nothing and looking at the floor. WHAT WOULD YOU SAY?

a. "If you don't see things my way, just say so." (S)
b. "If things don't sound the way to you they do to me, just say so." (H)
c. "If you don't feel the way I do about things, just say so." (T)
d. "If you don't share my opinions about this, just say so." (O)

Now, count up your choices and enter the totals here:

SIGHT ____ HEARING ____ TOUCH ____ OTHER ____

Seven or more in any one category indicates a clear preference for that Mode; a score of three or less indicates a clear *non*-preference. A set of scores such as SIGHT (5), HEARING (5), TOUCH (3), OTHER (2), would indicate a mixed SIGHT/HEARING PREFERENCE.

Additional Activities

TOUCH

SIGHT

HEARING

- What kind of things do you like to do best? Things that use your eyes, or things that use your ears? Things that mean using your hands a lot? Things that don't fit any of these categories? Make a list of your favorite pastimes and examine it for more information about your preferred Sensory Mode.

- If you need to learn new information and remember it, what works best for you? Reading about it? Hearing about it? Hands-on activities? Or something else? Suppose you wanted to learn Morse Code, for example; would you learn better by reading about it, listening to a tape about it, or just trying to *do* it by tapping a finger or pushing a button?

39

- After you come home from a party or meeting, stop for a few minutes and consider what you remember best about it. Things you saw? Things you heard? Things you felt? Something else?

- Close your eyes and imagine that you're at an ocean beach or a lake. Now—quick—what are you most aware of? Something you see? Something you hear? Something you feel? Something else?

Identifying
The Sensory Modes:
Which One
Is Being Used?

INSTRUCTIONS

Here are twenty sentences, each one constructed to express one of the three most common preferred Sensory Modes. Read each one and decide which Mode it presents; then write S for Sight, H for Hearing, or T for Touch in the parentheses at the end of the sentence. You'll find answers at the end of this section to check your work against.

1. MOTHER: "You don't understand at *all*. The picture you have of this situation isn't clear—it's completely distorted." ( )

2. BOSS: "This problem is *not* too hot to handle. It's rough, sure, but we can handle it." ( )

3. FRIEND: "Sure, you *say* you like me! But all the time you're giving me a bunch of static." ( )

4. SPOUSE: "You don't listen to me at all. I talk and talk, and you don't hear one word I say. You have both ears shut tight, all the time." ( )

5. SALESPERSON: "If I hear you right, this deal isn't exactly music to your ears. Is there anything I can do to make it sound better to you?" ( )

6. BOOR: "You don't like it, you can *lump* it. How does *that* grab you?" ( )

7. DENTIST: "I promise you—you won't feel a thing." ( )

8. COLLEAGUE: "I'm going to see if I can't shed a little light on this problem, so we can quit stumbling around in the dark." ( )

9. CHILD "All you do is *yell* at me! I can't hear myself *think*!" ( )

10. GROCER: "You see this box of rice here? It looks just like that other box, but it's camouflage. It's not the same at all." ( )

11. EXECUTIVE: "We'll never get anywhere with this negotiation if you people keep shoving every solid idea that comes along under the rug!" ( )

12. NEIGHBOR: "Her problem is, she's always been completely blind to her children's faults. She sees them as perfect, every one of them." ( )

13. STUDENT: "I've got this idea buzzing around in my head . . . you want to hear it?" ( )

14. TEACHER: "This course will give you a whole new perspective on math—an entirely different view of advanced algebra. I promise you." ( )

15. RELATIVE: "I *don't* look down on your side of the family. Don't be ridiculous. Maybe I don't picture them all as saints, like you do, but I don't look down on them." ( )

16. LAWYER: "First you have to grasp the essential facts in the case; then you try to handle all the minor details. That's the only way to tackle anything this complicated." ( )

17. NURSE: "I could hear the strain in his voice when he called, Doctor. He sounded very muffled and weak to me." ( )

18. PARENT: "I can't believe my eyes—is that hairdo really supposed to make her a vision of loveliness?" ( )

19. FATHER: "Could you give me a hand with this crate? I can't seem to get a decent grip on it." ( )

20. GARDENER: "The way I look at it, if you can't see yourself doing hard work you've got no business planting roses." ( )

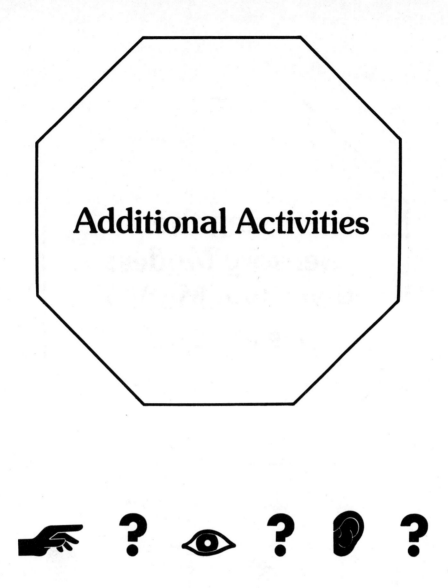

Additional Activities

- Just pay attention. While you're listening to the radio or television, keep a piece of paper and a pencil handy, and write down Sensory Mode vocabulary that you notice being used. (You won't want to write down every use of "see/hear/feel" and "look/listen/touch"; but writing down the less constant ones is good practice.)

- Use your junk mail. Before you throw it away, underline the Sensory Mode items and identify them as Sight, Hearing, or Touch. Do you see any patterns? Do sweepstakes offerings rely more on one Mode than another? What about insurance policy letters? Fund raiser letters?

- Try to notice Sensory Mode vocabulary used by people around you, in a discreet way. Can you clearly identify the preferred Modes of some of your family, friends, or associates? What about "mixed" Mode examples—do you hear anybody say things like "I see what you're saying" or "I hear the picture"?

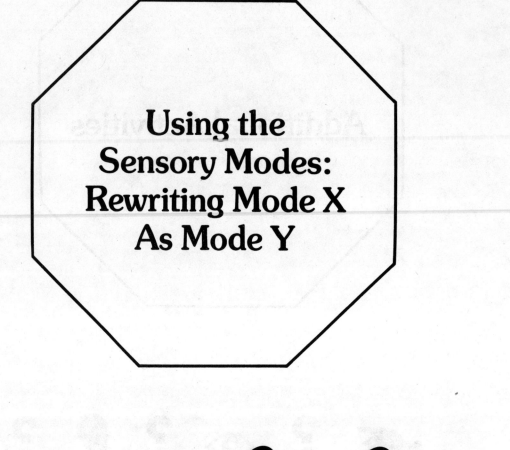

Using the Sensory Modes: Rewriting Mode X As Mode Y

INSTRUCTIONS

Here are fifteen sentences written to demonstrate a preference for one of the Sensory Modes. At the end of each one, you'll see either S for SIGHT, H for HEARING, or T for TOUCH— *rewrite the sequence in that Mode.* Don't worry if you can't get an exact match, because many times that isn't possible; just try to express the same meaning as closely as you can. Perfect sets such as "That looks good to me"/"That sounds good to me"/"That feels good to me" are rare. If you come to a part of the example that you just can't find a match for, substitute something that isn't from *any* of the Sensory Modes, to avoid a Mode mismatch. At the end of the section, you'll find a set of suggested answers; but there is no one "right" answer for these. (NOTE: In the first five examples, the Sensory Mode items have been italicized to help you get started.)

1. "No matter how *hard* I work at it, I just can't *put my finger* on the source of all the *bad feeling* in this office." (S) REWRITE IN SIGHT MODE.

   _____

   _____

2. "His summary *clearly reflects* the *haziness* of his judgment." (H) REWRITE IN HEARING MODE.

   _____

   _____

3. If you *listen* carefully when the information is presented, your perception of the issue will be free of *static* and *noise*." (S)

   _____

   _____

4. "Can't you *see* that when she *looks* at him she doesn't really *see* him—she only *sees* what she wants to *see*?" (H)

   _____

   _____

5. "If you always *focus* on everyone's faults, of course life will seem *gloomy* to you." (T) REWRITE IN TOUCH MODE.

   _____

   _____

6. "Our players' shining performance this season made everybody take a second look, and they changed their views of the team's potential." (T)

   _____

   _____

7. "The whole tone of the conversation was so depressing that I just couldn't listen to it." (T)

   _____

   _____

8. "I could just barely feel the terror of the slimy creature as it dragged itself through the thick underbrush." (S)

_____

_____

9. "If you push her over the edge, she's finally going to grasp the fact that you're only a bully." (S)

_____

_____

10. "Personally, I feel that my cousin is completely out of touch with reality." (S)

_____

_____

11. "Every single one of us can see clearly that we're working in the dark with this project." (T)

_____

_____

12. "If we don't all join in the chorus, it sounds to me like we'll all be fired." (T)

_____

_____

13. "My dad is really going to haul me over the coals—I can feel it coming." (H)

_____

_____

14. "I hear that the boss has decided to ring down the curtain on that crazy schedule." (T)

_____

_____

15. "It looks to me like your daughter is really blue." (T)

_____

_____

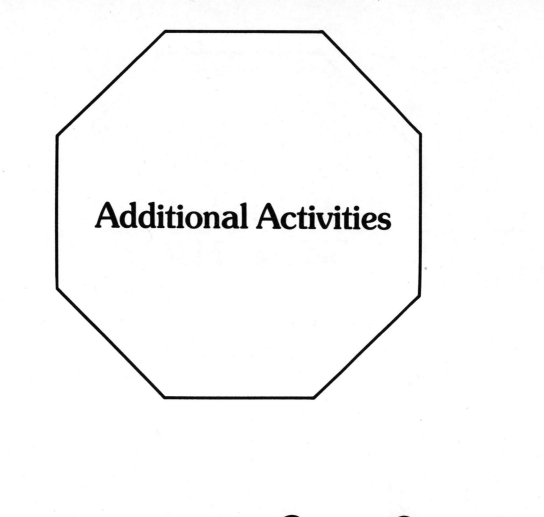

Additional Activities

- Try rewriting each of these in the *other* major Sensory Mode; try rewriting them in the more unusual vocabulary of Taste/Smell Modes. And try rewriting them all without using *any* Sensory Mode vocabulary items.
- Keep a small notebook where you enter items from each of the Sensory Modes as they occur to you or come your way, watching especially for those that have an approximately equivalent form in two or more Modes.

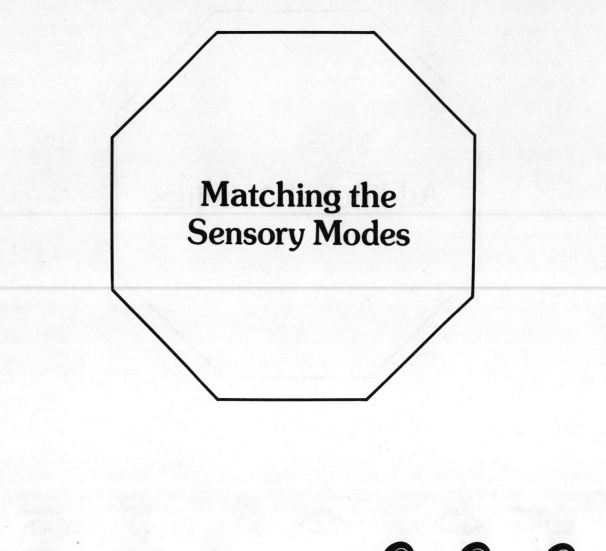

Matching the Sensory Modes

INSTRUCTIONS

Here are ten brief dialogues using the major Sensory Modes. In each one, three lines have been filled in but the fourth has been left blank for you to fill in. Write in a fourth line, matching the Sensory Mode that has been used in the other three lines. You'll find a set of suggested answers at the end of this section; again, there are no "right" answers.

DIALOGUE ONE:

Banker: "I'm sorry. Our bank is not willing to make you that loan. We just don't see it as a good risk."

Customer: "But I can show you that it *is* a good risk!"

Banker: "Look—we've made our decision."

Customer: "_____

_____ "

DIALOGUE TWO:

Patient: "I can't see spending $500 for just one test."

Doctor: "Look at it as an investment in your health."

Patient: "Doctor, I don't have an investor's point of view here! It's too much money."

Doctor: "_____

_____ "

DIALOGUE THREE:

Child: "You haven't heard a single word I've said!"

Parent: "Listen, that's not true. I've been all ears."

Child: "I don't believe you. You're only *pretending* to pay attention to me!"

Parent: "_____

_____ "

DIALOGUE FOUR:

Customer: "Don't you *dare* look at me like that! I don't have to shop here, you know!"

Salesperson: "I can see that you're angry."

Customer: "Well! Aren't *you* the eagle eye!"

Salesperson: "_____

_____ "

DIALOGUE FIVE:

Teacher: "You have *no grasp* of the principles of algebra!"

Student: "I feel the same way about it you do."

Teacher: "Well? Do you plan to take any firm steps to change the situation?"

Student: "_____

_____ "

DIALOGUE SIX:

Lawyer: "I have a strange feeling about this case of yours."
Client: "A good strange feeling or a bad one?"
Lawyer: "I'm not sure. I can't quite put my finger on it."

Client: "_____

_____"

DIALOGUE SEVEN:

Boss: "Tracy, some new facts about your performance have recently come to light."
Employee: "I see. Could you be more clear, please?"
Boss: Well . . . you seem to be under a cloud."

Employee: "_____

_____"

DIALOGUE EIGHT:

Clerk: "You have to sign on *both* lines, or there'll be all kinds of racket about it."
Citizen: "I hear you—no need to go on and on about it."
Clerk: "Sorry, but I'm the one people will yell at if you don't fill that out right."

Citizen: "_____

_____"

DIALOGUE NINE:

Grandparent: "Will you just look at that baby! Bright as a new penny!"
Neighbor: "She's the apple of your eye, isn't she?"
Grandparent: "Am I that transparent?"

Neighbor: "_____

_____"

DIALOGUE TEN:

Politician: "Your problems weigh heavily with me you know."
Citizen: "But you're not taking any *action*!"
Politician: "Please—keep a stiff upper lip, friend. We're working on the matter."

Citizen: "_____

_____"

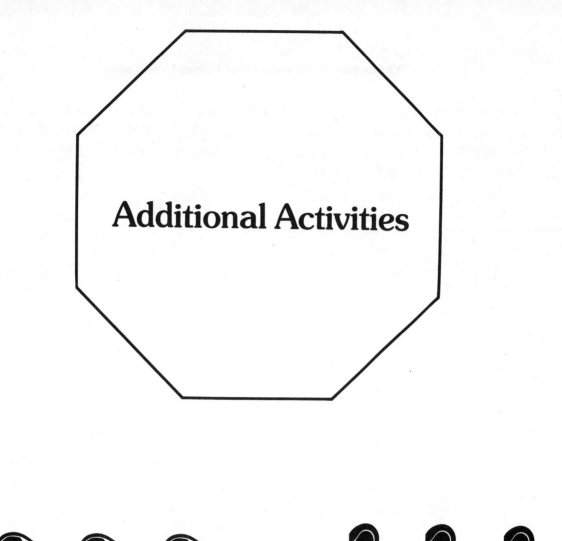

Additional Activities

- For a thorough workout in the use of the Sensory Modes, try rewriting all of these dialogues completely in the two Modes not already used for each one. When no vocabulary item exists to match a particular chunk of a sequence, substitute cognitive items (for example "think, understand, believe, know, in my opinion, to my mind" or other non-sensory material).

- Pay attention to some radio or television talk shows, especially those in which a single guest has to face a panel of reporters or other speakers. Don't try to write anything down, but try to become aware of (a) whether you are hearing Sensory Mode matching or mismatching, and (b) whether you can isolate negative or positive effects based on the match or mismatch. Any interview (for example on the morning news broadcasts, or "Sixty Minutes") will also give you opportunities for this kind of practice. Are there certain interviewers who seem to you to have deliberate strategies for matching or mismatching Sensory Modes? If so, what sort of results do they get that way?

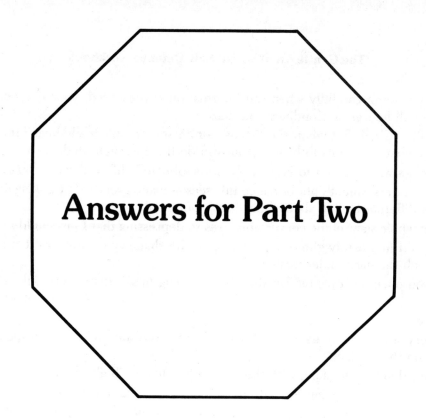

Answers for Part Two

A. IDENTIFYING THE SENSORY MODE

1. S	5. H	9. H	13. H	17. H
2. T	6. T	10. S	14. S	18. S
3. H	7. T	11. T	15. S	19. T
4. H	8. S	12. S	16. T	20. S

Note: Look again at example #7. This one doesn't really tell you anything about the person's Sensory Mode preferences; it's just something a dentist is expected to say. The therapist's "And how does that make you feel?" is a similar example; probably a teacher's use of "I see" is another one.

B. USING THE SENSORY MODES

1. "No matter how much I look at it, I just can't seem to see clearly what's causing all the bad feeling in this office."
   (NOTICE, there's no obvious replacement for "bad feeling" in Sight Mode. You could go to "discord" or "ill will" but there's no "bad seeing" to use.)
2. "The way his summary is garbled is clear evidence that his judgment is also distorted."

3. "If you watch carefully when the information is presented, your perception of the issue will be free of cloudiness and haze."

4. "Can't you tell that when she listens to him she doesn't really hear him—she only hears what she wants to hear?" (Can you do this in Touch Mode?)

5. "If you always grab on to everyone's faults, of course life will seem rough to you."

6. "Our players' smooth performance this season made everybody think again, and they got a different feeling about their team's potential."

7. "The whole slant of the conversation was so depressing that I just couldn't handle it."

8. "I could just barely glimpse the terror of the shadowy creature as it dragged itself through the dark underbrush."

9. "If you open her eyes too far, she's finally going to see that you're only a bully."

10. "Personally, it looks to me as though my cousin has completely lost sight of the real world."

11. "Every single one of us can feel perfectly well the way we're swimming against the tide on this project."

12. "If we don't all go along with the herd, I feel like we'll all be fired."

13. "My dad is really going to read me the riot act—I can already hear it coming."

14. "What I get from the grapevine is that the boss has decided to put an end to that crazy schedule."

15. "It feels to me like your daughter is really heavy-hearted."

C. MATCHING THE SENSORY MODES

1. "Well, I guess I'll have to look somewhere else for the money."
   OR "I think you ought to take another look at my application."

2. "Well, let's see if we can find a cheaper way to do it."
   "Try to see it my way—it's necessary."

3. "I'm sorry—tell me once more, and I promise to listen carefully."
   "Well, I'm listening now. Tell me again."

4. "I wonder if we could take another look at this situation."
   "Let's see if we can get a clearer picture of this problem."

5. "If I can just get a grip on it, I will."
   "I feel like I ought to at least try."

6. "Well, we can't go on with this until that's straightened out."
   "That does *not* make me feel confident!"

7. "From whose point of view?"
   "I don't look at it that way?"

8. "As I told you, I'm doing it like you said to do it."
   "Listen, I'll do it right—don't nag."

9. "Like a pane of glass."
   "Unless a person has their eyes shut, you are."

10. "Well, I don't know how much longer I can hold on."
    "I'll do my best, but it's really hard."

PART THREE:
The Verbal Attack Patterns: Recognition And Response

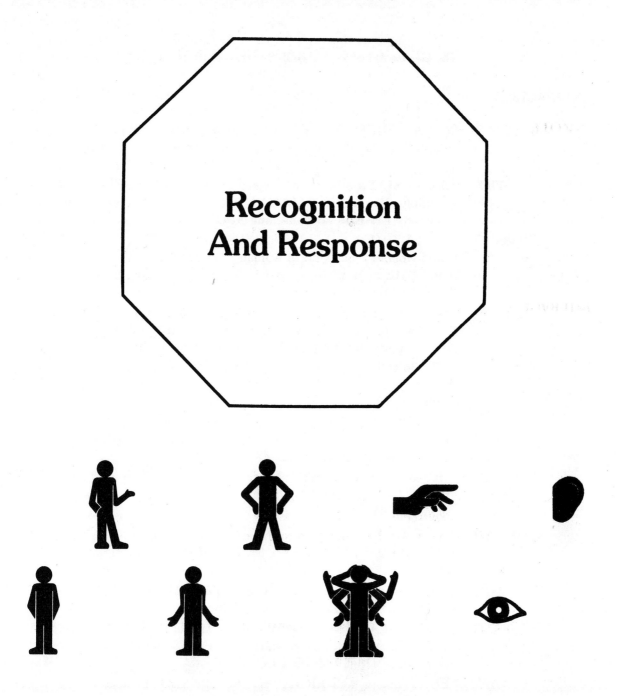

Recognition And Response

The interaction below is a typical argument between a husband and wife who communicate with one another badly. An example of a confrontation between a parent and child, or a teacher and student, or any other two individuals who might know each other well enough to really get into a row, would serve the purpose. But a husband/wife example is a good choice because (a) the attacks don't have to be subtle, and (b) there's no difference of rank between the speakers that has to be taken into account. Start by reading the dialogue all the way through; then go on to the instructions that follow. You'll find answers, and suggested answers, at the end of the chapter.

INTERACTION

HUSBAND: "GOOD GRIEF! Will you just LOOK at this place? What if somebody came OVer? Don't you even CARE if people know we LIVE LIKE THIS?"

WIFE: "If it REALLY bothered you, you'd clean it up yourSELF, instead of spending all your time MAKING the messes and then waiting for somebody ELSE to do something ABOUT them!"

HUSBAND: "Oh, I WOULD, would I? That's how you FEEL, is it? SOME men would wonder what kind of woman they'd MARried if she talked like that! SOME men might wonder if their wives had lost their MINDS if they heard them talk like that!"

WIFE: "WHY do you always start carrying on like this, EVERY single Saturday morning? EVen a man with no sensitivity at ALL should be able to figure out that it RUINS the whole weekEND!"

HUSBAND: "Why do YOU always put off CLEANing till *Sat*urday, if you don't want the weekend ruined? Tell me THAT! A woman with any sense at ALL would REalize that after a man works HARD all week he likes to get up to some peace and QUIet on Saturday morning!"

WIFE: "If you really LOVED me, you wouldn't WANT me to spend all my time scrubbing and vacuuming!"

HUSBAND: "Oh, come on! You don't spend five minutes a DAY doing that stuff!"

WIFE: "You know—everybody underSTANDS why you're such a faNATic about HOUSEwork, my dear."

HUSBAND: "What is THAT supposed to mean? I'm a fanatic? JUST BECAUSE I WANT TO LIVE LIKE A DECENT HUMAN BEing, that makes me a faNATIC?"

WIFE: "WHY do you always have to keep yelling like that? Don't you even CARE if the neighbors hear you RAVING like a MANIAC?"

HUSBAND: "FIRST I'M A LUNatic, NOW I'm a MANiac! Look, just you go right ahead and do whatever you want to do! I'm not going to stay here and listen to you ONE MINUTE LONGer!"

WIFE: "FINE! You just go RIGHT AHEAD and LEAVE! That's what you always do ANyway, whether I clean or NOT."

HUSBAND: "If you REALLY cared anything about me, you wouldn't WANT to drive me out of my own home every weekend!"

WIFE: "I do NOT drive you out of your home! I knock myself out to plan a pleasant weekend for you in this house, and you ALways manage to SPOIL it! I'm not driving you ANYwhere—you are leaving of your OWN FREE WILL! And I wish you would quit talking about it and go on and DO it!"

HUSBAND: "FINE! I'm ON MY WAY!"

WIFE: "FINE!"

The Verbal Attack Patterns:

INSTRUCTIONS

1. Count up the number of examples of Verbal Attack Patterns from the Octagon in this interaction and write it here. _____ (See page 17, *The Gentle Art of Verbal Self-Defense*)

2. In each attack you find, underline the words that carry the bait. Then write down, on a separate sheet of paper, what the speaker intended those words to MEAN. Finally, write down the *presupposed* attacks for each example. For instance, the first one is "Don't you even CARE if people know we LIVE LIKE THIS?" The words to be underlined would be "we LIVE LIKE THIS"; and the speaker intends that bait to mean, "The way we live is repulsive and disgusting and horrible." The presupposed attacks are "Any decent person WOULD care, but you don't, so you're a creep."

3. Now let's see if we can do something to improve the linguistic environment in which this couple lives. Since every language interaction is a feedback process, with each response depending on the utterance that comes before it, we can't change *any* part of the dialogue without having to change all of it. There are an infinite number of possible changes for each utterance, with an infinite number of corresponding possible changes for each response. In the sequences below, blank lines have been left for you to write in appropriate responses to the attacks, using the techniques described in THE GENTLE ART. There are no "right" answers, but you'll find suggested ones at the end of the chapter.

REVISION ONE

  HUSBAND: "GOOD GRIEF! Will you just LOOK at this place? What if somebody came OVER? Don't you even CARE if people know we LIVE LIKE THIS?"

    WIFE: "_____

      _____"

REVISION TWO

    WIFE: "If you really LOVED me, you wouldn't WANT me to spend all my time scrubbing and vacuuming!"

  HUSBAND: "_____

      _____"

REVISION THREE

    WIFE: "If it REALLY bothered you, you'd clean it up yourself (etc.)"

  HUSBAND: "_____

      _____"

REVISION FOUR

HUSBAND: "SOME men would wonder if . . . (etc.)

WIFE: "You're absolutely right."

HUSBAND: "I am? What do you mean by THAT?"

WIFE: "_____

_____"

REVISION FIVE

WIFE: "WHY do you always start carrying on like this (etc.)"

HUSBAND: "Okay, how about if I start writing it down when I have something I want to gripe about? And then you could write me an answer."

WIFE: "That sounds like an awful lot of TROUBLE!"

HUSBAND: "_____

_____"

REVISION SIX

HUSBAND: "A woman with any sense at ALL would REalize . . . (etc.)"

WIFE: "_____

_____"

REVISION SEVEN

WIFE: "Don't you even CARE if the neighbors hear you RAVING . . . (etc.)?"

HUSBAND: "No."

WIFE: "What? You can't be serious!"

HUSBAND: "_____

_____"

REVISION EIGHT

HUSBAND: "If you REALLY cared anything about me, you wouldn't WANT to drive me out . . . (etc.)"

WIFE: "Honey, when did you start thinking I don't care about you?"

HUSBAND: "Yesterday afternoon, THAT'S when—when you told my sister that you thought her kids were spoiled brats."

WIFE: "_____

_____"

The Verbal Attack Patterns:

REVISION NINE

      WIFE: "WHY do you always have to keep yelling like that?"

    HUSBAND: "_____

_____"

REVISION TEN

    HUSBAND: "SOME men would wonder what kind of woman they'd MARried if . . . (etc.)"

      WIFE: "I'm SURE they would. Absolutely!"

    HUSBAND: "Hey—I was talking about YOU!"

      WIFE: "_____

_____"

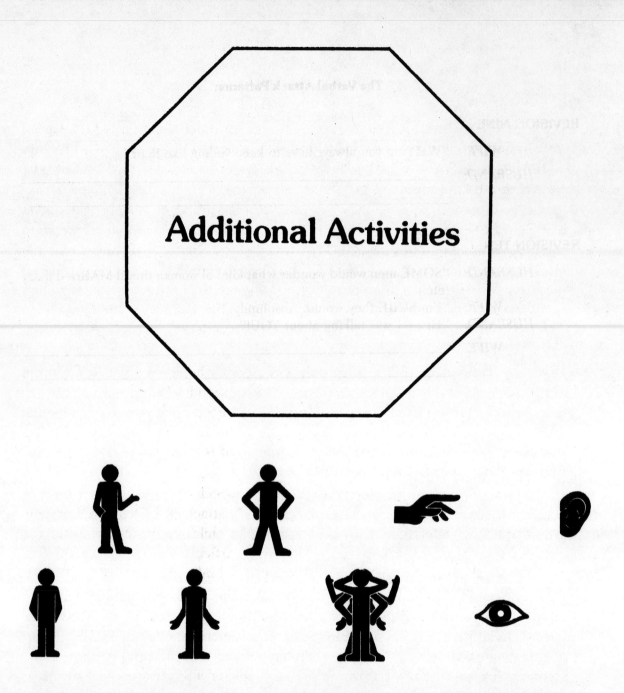

Additional Activities

• The example above was a husband/wife confrontation. Try rewriting it for each of the following:

a. A parent, and a teenage child who is supposed to do a substantial share of the household chores.

b. Two friends of the same gender who share an apartment and are supposed to do equal shares of the housework.

c. Two salespeople who share an office and are supposed to do equal shares of the work in their department.

You'll have to allow for the fact that (a) the parent outranks and can punish the child; (b) the two friends depend on each other, because neither one could afford to rent the apartment alone; and (c) the salespeople have to keep on working together, but they don't have to *live* together. (You might also rewrite the interaction as it would go if the speakers were a husband and wife, but the wife also held a fulltime job outside the home.)

- Select a situation in your own life that you feel uneasy about . . . your relationship with your boss, or your father, or your doctor . . . anyone you consistently seem to have trouble communicating with. Write a dialogue between yourself and the other person in that situation. Begin by trying to write the worst row you can possibly produce. Use all the Attack Patterns; ignore the presuppositions; respond to all the bait. Do everything you can to make the fight worse. When you've constructed as hostile and confrontational an interaction as you can possibly can, try to fix it.

- Pay close attention to your own speech, to find out whether you yourself use the Verbal Attack patterns from the Octagon. (Enlist a friend or relative or associate to help with this, if you like.) Every time you hear yourself using one, make a mental note to remember as much as you can of the interaction; then later decide what you could have said *instead* of the attack. Your goal is to eliminate these patterns from your language behavior completely.

- In the same way, watch for these patterns in the speech of others. Does it seem to you that there is any tendency toward a particular attack on the part of a specific group, such as women, or the elderly, or young children? Is there one of the patterns that seems to turn up more often in a particular situation, regardless of the characteristics of the speaker? Watch for useful information.

- Collect examples of the Attack Patterns from the mass media. (For instance, advertisements that begin with "If you REALLY want good taste/care about your family's health . . . "or "If your auto repair store/supermarket really CARES about keeping your business . . . " Notice what happens on television and in films: if one character uses an Attack Pattern, does the character who answers take the bait? Listen to people who have society's permission to criticize you—your minister or priest or rabbi, your doctor or dentist or therapist, etc. Do they use the Octagon sequences when they talk to you, or to a group that you're part of? HOW HIGH is the level of this particular kind of pollution in your personal linguistic environment?

- When you realize that you're about to use one of the Attack Patterns, deliberately substitute a version with the strong stresses in the wrong places. For example, you are about to say to your daughter, "Don't you even CARE if your hair looks like a bird had built a nest in it?"; substitute, "Don't you even care IF YOUR HAIR looks like A bird had built a nest in IT?" What happens—how does the listener react?

- There are undoubtedly more of these patterns than the eight that are presented in

THE GENTLE ART. Start watching for new ones, and make a note of them when they come along. Then handle them just like the first eight. Ignore the bait; respond to the presupposition.

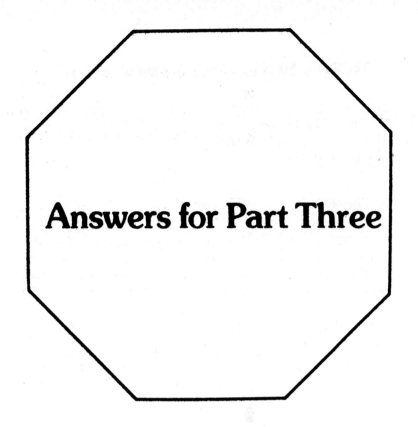

Answers for Part Three

1. Thirteen. (And a number of near misses!)

2. Here are the baits, with their intended meanings, and the presupposed attacks.

    a. *bait/meaning* (Done for you on page 59)

    a. *attack* (Done on page 59, as example.)

    b. *bait/meaning* For "If it REALLY bothered you, etc."—underline the whole sequence from "spending all your time MAKING the messes" to the end of the sentence. The speaker intends this to mean, "You are the one who gets the house dirty, not me, but you expect ME to get it *clean*."

    b. *attack* "You don't care how dirty the house is—it doesn't really bother you."

    c. *bait/meaning* For "SOME men would wonder what kind of woman, etc."—underline "she talked like that." The intended meaning is, "What you just said was really awful and disgraceful."

    c. *attack* "I'm a very superior man who is *above* wondering anything like that, and that's lucky for you; you should feel very grateful to me for being so unique and remarkable."

    d. *bait/meaning* For "SOME men might wonder if their wives, etc."—underline *two* chunks of bait, "wives had lost their MINDS" and "talk like that." The intended meaning is, "What you just said is the kind of thing people say who have lost their minds, so you sound as if you had lost yours."

    d. *attack* (Same as "c" above.)

e. *bait/meaning* For "WHY do you always start carrying on, etc."—underline "carrying on like this." The intended meaning is "The way you behave ('carry on') is horrible and stupid and has everything wrong with it."

e. *attack* "You ALways and without exception start carrying on every Saturday morning."

f. *bait/meaning* For "EVen a man with no sensitivity at ALL" and "it RUINS the whole weekEND"; the intended meanings for this double-baited attack are "You are completely insensitive" and "What you do makes the whole weekend horrible."

f. *attack* "This is so easy to figure out that it's hardly worth mentioning, and only somebody as inferior and insensitive as you are could possibly have any *trouble* figuring it *out*."

g. *bait/meaning* For "Why do YOU always put off CLEANing, etc."—underline "YOU always put off CLEANing till *Saturday*." The intended meaning is not only just what the sequence says, but also "All week long, when you *should* be cleaning, you just put it off and put it off."

g. *attack* "You have a reason for always and without exception putting off cleaning till Saturday—and that's what you always do."

h. *bait/meaning* For "A woman with any sense at ALL, etc."—underline "A woman with any sense at ALL." The intended meaning is "You are a woman who has no sense at all."

h. *attack* "You don't have any sense."

i. *bait/meaning* For "If you really LOVED me, you wouldn't WANT me to spend all my time, etc."—underline "spend all my time scrubbing and vacuuming." The wife intends that as a claim that that *is* how she spends all her time.

i. *attack* "You don't really love me." and "You are capable of controlling your wants and desires, if you'd just decide to do that."

j. *bait/meaning* For "You know—everybody underSTANDS, etc."—underline "you're such a faNATic about HOUSEwork." It means exactly that.

j. *attack* "You think the reason that you're a fanatic about housework is a secret, but it's not—everybody knows what it is, and everybody thinks it's terrible."

k. *bait/meaning* For "WHY do you always have to keep yelling, etc."—underline "yelling like that." The intended meaning is, "The way you yell and the length of time you spend yelling are completely awful and inexcusable."

k. *attack* "You always and without exception yell and yell like that, and you have a reason for doing so; I want to know what it is."

l. *bait/meaning* For "Don't you even CARE if the neighbors, etc."—underline "RAVING like a MANIAC." The intended meaning is, "The way you behave, verbally, sounds like the way a maniac raves."

l. *attack* "Any decent person would care if the neighbors heard them raving like a maniac, but you don't—so you're a creep."

m. *bait/meaning* For "If you REALLY cared anything about me, etc."—underline "drive me out of my own home every weekend," and the speaker is claiming that that is what his wife does.

m. *attack* "You don't really care anything about me."

3. Here are the suggestions for revisions.

ONE: "When did you start thinking that our friends will judge us by the way we keep house?"

TWO: "Of *course* I love you; I love you very much."

THREE: "Honey, it really does bother me—a LOT. (Or "When did you start thinking that I don't care if the house is a mess?"

FOUR: "I mean I agree with you, and I'd be interested in your opinions about a situation like that."

FIVE: "Okay. Then we don't have to do it." Or "You're probably right; it wasn't a very good idea."

SIX: "I couldn't agree with you more." Or "You're right; what amazes ME is that scientists that can put a man on the moon can't design a quiet vacuum cleaner."

SEVEN: "The idea that your neighbors are always listening to what's going on at your house is interesting—but frankly, I don't think they pay any attention." Or "When did you start thinking we had nosey neighbors, honey?"

EIGHT: "I hear you. Okay—let's talk about that." Or "So *that's* the problem! No wonder you're upset."

NINE: "I think it's because I forget my manners. What do you think?" (Or almost anything at all, *very softly*.)

TEN: "Oh, I'm sorry, honey. What was the problem?"

PART FOUR:
What Did X
Say / Do Wrong?

What Did X Say/Do Wrong?

INSTRUCTIONS

Here are ten language interactions in which the speakers make a variety of bad moves, using language behaviors identified in THE GENTLE ART as inefficient or ineffective or confrontational. (For instance: failing to match Sensory Modes; matching Satir Modes when it's not a good idea to do so; using body language, or mannerisms, that provoke negative reactions; using attacks from the Octagon.) After each interaction you'll find the speakers' names, followed by blank lines where you can write down what you feel has gone wrong. **The first one has been done for you as an example.

INTERACTION ONE

The scene is a business lunch at a restaurant. The speakers are two women and a man, all in their early thirties, who work for the same firm and have roughly equal rank. They are discussing plans for a new advertising campaign for one of their products.

YOLANDA: "All right, that's my proposal. Now—how about some input from you two?"

CARL: "Yolanda, everybody underSTANDS why this is so important to YOU. But to be perfectly frank, I think the whole idea is naive."

YOLANDA: "You'll have to give me some reasons for that, Carl— but not yet. First, I want to hear what *Janet* has to say."

JANET: "Well . . . I don't know. You're kind of putting me on the spot, aren't you? I mean, I don't really know—"

CARL: "THERE you go! Your standard wishy-washy female in action! Listen, Yolanda—*Janet* doesn't know, but I DO know. And WHAT I do know is this: it's a half-baked plan that will never WORK. Case closed."

JANET: "You interRUPTed me, Carl! You did NOT have to do THAT. I CERtainly wasn't going to take up THAT much of your precious time! But you couldn't STOOP to the basic courtesy of letting me finish what I had to SAY, *could* you? SO— I am going to vote with YoLANda!"

YOLANDA: *She makes no bad moves in this interaction.*

CARL: *He uses a Verbal Attack Pattern; he interrupts Janet; he makes a sexist remark; and he uses Blamer Mode much of the time.*

JANET: *She uses the language behavior patterns that our culture associates with children and intimidated subordinates.*

INTERACTION TWO

In this interaction the speakers are a husband and wife, eating lunch together at home.

HE: "Honey, I really need to talk to you about that bank loan. It sounds pretty good, but I'm not sure we ought to do it."

SHE: "There's something wrong with this potato salad. It *really* has a funny color to it."

**NOTE: One of the interactions is a ringer—it has no bad moves. Watch for that one.

> *HE:* "Honey . . . like I told you, the loan's not complicated. I just need to get you to listen to a couple of things here."
>
> *SHE:* "John, look at this stuff, will you? Don't you think it's gone bad?"
>
> *HE:* "No. I don't. I think it's fine."
>
> *SHE:* "Really? You mean you can't see that it's spoiled? Honestly . . . men have no sense of taste at all."
>
> *HE:* "Then WHY the BLAZES did you ask ME about the stupid potato salad?"
>
> *SHE:* "My goodness! WHY are yoU SNAPping at me like that?"
>
> *HE:* "_____
> _____"
>
> *SHE:* "_____
> _____"

INTERACTION THREE

This one takes place in a doctor's office. The doctor is male, in his late thirties; the patient is a woman of sixty.

> *WOMAN:* "Well, doctor, did you find anything?"
>
> *DOCTOR:* "No, Ellen, I didn't. Not a thing, I'm happy to say."
>
> *WOMAN:* "Then why do I *feel* like this?"
>
> *DOCTOR:* "Ellen—it's nothing to worry about. You have a mild somatization disorder."
>
> *WOMAN:* "Oh! Then you *did* find something! What—"
>
> *DOCTOR:* "Now, what you need to do is stop at the desk on your way out and make an appointment to come in again in a couple of months." (He picks up her chart and heads for the door.)
>
> *WOMAN:* "Doctor, I know you're busy, but—"
>
> *DOCTOR:* (He stops with his hand on the doorknob and glances at her quickly over his shoulder.) "I'll see you then, Ellen. Call me if you have any problems." (He leaves without looking back.)
>
> *DOCTOR:* "_____
> _____"
>
> *WOMAN:* "_____
> _____"

INTERACTION FOUR

The setting is a living room in an ordinary home, where three men (about the same age and rank) are watching a football game. They're neighbors, and they spend quite a lot of time this way. Suddenly the TV set just quits, right in the middle of the action.

GEORGE: "*Hey*! What happened?"

PHIL: "The TV went off, that's what happened."

GEORGE: "Well, I can SEE that! For crying out loud, WHAT IS IT about you, Phil, always taking everything everybody says LITerally? YOU know what I mean!"

BOB: "Do you two guys ALWAYS have to fight? Don't you even CARE if everybody else has to sit around on their thumbs while you act like a couple of stupid little kids?"

PHIL: "Meanwhile, back at the TV set . . . "

GEORGE: "It's YOUR SET, Philip—why don't you take a LOOK at it and see what's WRONG?"

PHIL: "I hear you, George old buddy, I *hear* you!"

GEORGE: "You don't LOOK like you hear me!"

BOB: "Hey, we're missing the GAME! Anybody that sits around ARguing, instead of going ahead and fixing the SET, just doesn't really CARE about football!"

GEORGE: "_____"

PHIL: "_____"

BOB: "_____"

INTERACTION FIVE

Here we have a young man who has gone to see an exhibit of modern sculpture at a museum. The guard for the exhibit is a middle-aged woman. The young man and the guard are the speakers.

GUARD: "Welcome to the Dintorizettino Exhibit. Touching the sculptures is not allowed."

MAN: "I don't want to touch them, ma'am. I just want to *look* at them."

GUARD: "Many people are unaware that sculpture can be damaged by handling, just like any other kind of art."

MAN: "I promise you I won't touch them."

GUARD: "Even a very YOUNG person should be able to understand that MASterpieces are not intended to be HANDled."

MAN: "Is that so? Well, this is ONE young person who has had eNOUGH, thank you! You just stand right there and see to it that this so-called

PUBLIC museum is protected from everybody under the age of *sixty*! And I'LL go somewhere where the word 'exhibit' means that you're able to look at the art in PEACE!"

GUARD: "_____
_____ "

MAN: "_____
_____ "

INTERACTION SIX

Two cars have pulled up side by side at a red light, with their windows down, waiting for the light to change. The drivers are both young; one is male, one female. There are no other cars in sight in any direction.

WOMAN: "That light must be broken! WHY does this kind of thing ALways happen to ME?"

MAN: "If you think it's broken, why don't you go on through it?"

WOMAN: "No—you go ahead. You got here first."

MAN: "What difference does it make who got here first?: There's plenty of room on the road for both of us. You go ahead."

WOMAN: "You're only saying that so if there's a poLICEman waiting around, I'LL be the one that gets the ticket instead of YOU!"

MAN: "WHAT??"

WOMAN: (She puts her head down on her arms on the steering wheel, and sighs loudly, then looks up at him again.) "I can't believe I said that."

MAN: "Oh, THAT'S all right. Don't worry about it. People are ALways insulting me—what's one insult more or less? It doesn't bother me."

WOMAN: "I'm SORry! I didn't *mean* to be insulting. I mean, I KNOW it wasn't a very nice thing to SAY, and I probably shouldn't have SAID it, but there's no reason to get inSULTED about it!"

MAN: "In my opinion, when somebody really goes out of his way to be nice, the other person could at LEAST—OH, NEVER mind!"

WOMAN: "_____
_____ "

MAN: "_____
_____ "

INTERACTION SEVEN

Here we have Mary and John, a typical young couple convinced that they are in love. Both of their sets of parents are having big Thanksgiving dinners; the young people have to decide which dinner to go to. Mary's parents are wealthy professionals; John comes from a working class background. They've already been discussing this for a while, and are beginning to lose their tempers.

MARY: "Look, sweetheart—there's no reason for us to argue about this. It's ridiculous, and I know how to settle it. Let's just go to *your* folks' place for Thanksgiving."

JOHN: "You're KIDding! Would you really do that, just like that? That sounds *great*! But what'll you tell your parents?"

MARY: (She shrugs her shoulders.) "I'll just tell them the *truth*, John. That I love you far too much to ruin your family's holiday just to spare their feelings. MY parents are capable of underSTANDing these things."

JOHN: (He is silent, briefly.) "Now wait a minute. What does THAT mean?"

MARY: "I don't see what you're getting at, darling."

JOHN: "OH yes you do!"

MARY: "All right, John. What do YOU think I mean?"

JOHN: (He folds his arms over his chest and scowls at her.) "First, you mean that going to my folks' house is going to really hurt YOUR folks. And you mean I don't love YOU enough to be willing to hurt MY folks. But YOUR parents are such superior people that THEY can *han*dle it, right? Right? That makes YOU really noble, and your FOLKS really noble, and all that jazz! And you're making ME and MY folks sound like some kind of LOWlifes! That's what you mean—I'M not deaf! And you better stop and think your little snob power play *over*, lady. Because I am NOT the kind of wimp you can pull a stunt like THAT on!"

MARY: She raises her eyebrows and looks him right in the eye.) "Oh, REALLy! How INteresting. Tell me, John—what kind of wimp ARE you?"

MARY: "_____
_____"

JOHN: "_____
_____"

INTERACTION EIGHT

In this interaction, the speakers are a male factory worker in his late twenties and his middle-aged foreman. The worker is trying to convince the foreman that the company's decision to close 100 spaces in the parking lot and ask the employees to carpool is a very bad idea.

WORKER: "Ed, I wish you'd try to get a better grasp of the way we all feel about this parking lot business. Everybody on my shift felt like I ought to talk to you about it."

FOREMAN: "There's not really anything to say, Louis. I just work here; I don't make decisions about parking lots. Management says we close it, we close it."

WORKER: "But you could *talk* to them about it, right?"

FOREMAN: "Maybe. If I had something to say that made sense."

WORKER: "Ed, the way we feel, this is just like some kind of a natural disaster. Like a tornado, you know? Car pooling, we'll all be crammed in together in our cars like sardines in a can, and fighting all the time about who forgot to buy the gas and whether we can stop someplace to pick up somebody's kid—it would never *work*, Ed. It's like this tornado just came roaring down out of the sky, when nobody was ex*pecting* it."

FOREMAN: "And the wind was so bad it jammed you all into a little tiny sardine can, right?"

WORKER: "Now, Ed, *I* didn't say that. WHY are you always putting words in my mouth and trying to make me look stupid?"

FOREMAN: "Louis, I want to tell you something. You know sardines? They're dead. They don't CARE how crowded it gets in the can. And they don't GRIPE about it. Not even in a tornado!" (He walks away, chuckling to himself and shaking his head.)

WORKER: "_____
_____"

FOREMAN: "_____
_____"

INTERACTION NINE

Sarah is an elderly woman living in a retirement home. She's convinced that people there dislike her, and she's feeling threatened. During a visit from a young niece she mentions her concern, and the niece helps her draw a Verbal Network Power Diagram so that they can get a clear picture of the situation. They can then see that Sarah has only two people to be concerned about. One is an employee who is always "forgetting" to do things if anybody annoys her in any way; the second is a woman resident who is planning to move in about three months, but who now spends much of her day trying to run Sarah's life.

NIECE: "Aunt Sarah, you know what I'd do if I were you? I'd report the maid to the manager, first of all, and I'd keep right on reporting her every time she pulled that 'forgetting' trick."

AUNT: "It wouldn't do any good."

NIECE: "It might. Even a man like your manager ought to be able to handle a problem like that. Either the maid cuts it out or she finds another job—*that's* not complicated. As for Mrs. Blesser ... Aunt Sarah, can't you just ignore her for three months? Just stay away from her?"

AUNT: "I guess maybe I could. When she comes around sticking her nose in my business I could just act like I don't even hear her. Sure. If I do that, she'll give up and go bother somebody else."

NIECE: "Right! She'll get the idea, if you do that—it won't be any fun to lean on you any more. And then she'll be gone."

AUNT: "It's not as bad as I thought. I don't know why I got so upset."

NIECE: "You got upset because you didn't have anybody to go over all this stuff with, that's all. I don't blame you one bit. But you've got it all under control now."

AUNT: "_____
_____"

NIECE: "_____
_____"

INTERACTION TEN

Here we have three speakers: Jeanne, a young woman who feels very sick and is scared that she may be having a heart attack; her older sister (Leslie), who thinks that's nonsense; and the sister's husband (Sam), who is caught in the middle.

LESLIE: "Really, Jeanne, can't you calm down a little? You're getting yourself all excited over nothing."

JEANNE: "Leslie, I don't think so. I feel so strange ... I think something is really wrong."

LESLIE: "Nonsense! Anybody as young as YOU are that thinks she's having a heart attack needs her HEAD examined, not her HEART!"

SAM: "For crying out loud, Leslie, are you going to sit here and watch your own sister die right before your EYES? Just to win an ARGUMENT?"

LESLIE: "WELL, Jeanne, I hope you're HAPPY now! You have managed to make my husband speak to me in a way that he has NEVER spoken to me before, and—Oh, for heaven's SAKE! Are you going to CRY, NOW? I can't beLIEVE you would stoop to such melodramatics over a little indigestion! If you didn't EAT so much, Jeanne Marie, you wouldn't HAVE indigestion! And I, for one—"

JEANNE: "Sam, please. Please help me."

LESLIE: "Sam, she's faked this kind of stuff her whole life long, ever since she was a baby! Even a MAN ought to be able to see through THAT act!"

SAM: "Shut up, Leslie."

LESLIE: "WHAT DID YOU SAY TO ME?"

SAM: "I said shut up. NOW. I'm calling an ambulance."

What Did X Say / Do Wrong?

JEANNE: "_____
_____"

LESLIE: "_____
_____"

SAM: "_____
_____"

79

Additional Activities

- Choose a brief sequence of language to work with, such as "I like you a lot" or "it's been a pleasure to talk with you" or "that's a good idea" . . . something short and easily remembered. Now practice using that sequence with different stress patterns, different tones of voice, different intonations, and different kinds of body language. Try to make it sound like each of the Satir Modes in turn; try to make it express lots of different emotional messages; try to make it a verbal attack and then an expression of affection and then a bored remark by someone who is feeling no other emotion. Just be sure you don't change the words themselves in any way. If you want to work on this with a friend, take turns, with one of you using the sequence and the other trying to spot what the speaker is doing. (This is a standard activity used to teach acting, by the way.)

• Play the game of "Linguistic Pollution." Get together with a friend or two and act out the role-playing scenarios listed below, doing everything you possibly can to pollute the linguistic environment as you go along. Here is a list of potential sources of such pollution you can use:

a. Always mismatch the Sensory Mode that comes at you.
b. Always choose the worst possible Satir Mode for the situation.
c. Use verbal attack patterns whenever you can.
d. When you hear verbal attack patterns, always ignore presuppositions and respond vigorously to the bait.
e. Mix up your metaphors.
f. Use Hedges frequently.

(You will be able to think of other language-toxins to use; this is certainly not a complete list. However, don't use open insults such as obscenities or elitist remarks or culturally loaded vocabulary—when you do that it becomes too easy for people to get hurt. Furthermore, it is a waste of your time, since those things require no skill at all.)

Role-playing scenarios to use:

a. One person is a bank loan officer; another is applying for a two thousand dollar signature loan (a loan with no security or collateral behind it). If you have more than two people, others can be relatives of the applicant.
b. One person is a lawyer interviewing applicants for a fileclerk's job; another is an applicant for the job who is overqualified because he or she has a master's degree in English literature. If you need extras, they can be other partners in the law firm.
c. One person is a police officer; another is a driver stopped for starting through an intersection just before a red light turned green; extras can be passengers in the car.
d. One person is an employee at the "returns & exchanges" counter in a fancy department store; another is a customer returning a gadget that doesn't work properly. Extras can be friends accompanying the customer, or other customers in the line.

• Start looking actively for the linguistic toxic waste dumps in your own life. Make a list of them, and rank them from the most dangerous to the least dangerous. (A sample list might include: your workplace; the house of a relative who always makes you feel depressed and miserable; a television show you watch regularly because other family members like it, but that you feel contains much linguistic garbage; a restaurant you go to because it is convenient and inexpensive, but where the staff is verbally unpleasant; and an area of the health care system where you are a consumer.) Choose one of the dumps on your list and do two things. First, give it another chance, paying close attention to the language interactions you observe there—is it really as bad as you had thought it was? If the answer is yes, begin using your verbal self-defense skills in a cleanup effort; if the answer is no, take it off your list and choose a different dump to work on.

- Set up for yourself a "language behavior notebook." (You can do this in written form, or on casette tapes, or in your computer—whatever is most comfortable and convenient for you.) Use it as a place to store all the information you've been collecting about your linguistic environment as you went through this workbook. Divide it into sections that will be useful for you. Here's a list of possible section titles to get you started; you will be able to think of lots of others to add, according to what parts of the linguistic environment interest you most and need the most attention in your life.

a. Language Behavior Profiles For People I Know. (Here you would list information like the following: a person's name and brief identifying description; preferred Satir Mode; preferred sensory mode; favorite attack patterns, if any; observations of your own about that person's body language or voice quality; preferred personal space—that is, how far away from the speaker he/she likes to be during language interactions; your observations about the person's listening behavior; special facts, such as your knowledge that the person's native language is French rather than English.)
b. My Own Language Behavior Profile. (Same as above, but for yourself. It would be a good idea to do this every six months or so, to see if you observe changes. This is a good place for you to record the work you do on your voice quality, and the changes that you—and others—notice.)
c. Language Behavior In The Media.
d. Journal Pages. (Like those on pages 76–79 in *The Gentle Art*, where you can record language interactions you participate in, what you really said and what you think you should have said, etc.)
e. Examples Of Good Metaphors For Future Use.
f. Examples Of Body Language That I React To Negatively.
g. Examples Of Body Language That I React To Positively.
h. Changes I Want To Make In My Own Language Behavior.
i. Verbal Attack Patterns And Responses. (For entering new attack patterns, and your ideas for effective responses, as you discover them.)

j. Language Behavior Patterns I Have Noticed. (For entering information you discover about language behavior patterns that seem to sort themselves out according to the sexual gender of speakers, or their ages, or other characteristics.)

k. Linguistic Toxic Waste Dumps.

l. Clippings, References, Quotations, Etc.

m. Language Games, Puzzles, Etc.

n. Language Behavior Problems To Work On.

o. Miscellaneous.

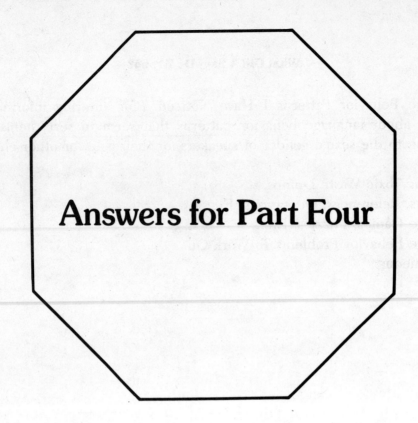

Answers for Part Four

Here are the analyses of bad moves in the interactions. (The first one has been done for you on page 72.)

INTERACTION TWO

> *HE:* He insists on using Hearing Mode, even though his wife uses Sight Mode only; if he'd switched to Sight Mode he might have been able to get her attention. When he runs out of patience, he goes straight to Blamer Mode and attacks her.
>
> *SHE:* Like her husband, she is mismatching the Sensory Modes, using Sight Mode to his Hearing Mode. She is not listening to him at all. She makes a sexist remark. And when he justifiably loses his temper, she responds to his Blaming with more Blaming.

INTERACTION THREE

> *DOCTOR:* He addresses Ellen by her first name, even though she addresses him by his title and is a good deal older than he is. He gives her several contradictory messages. He uses jargon that she doesn't understand. He walks out and leaves her, without answering her questions or

explaining, although it's obvious that she's not through talking to him. His body language clearly says, "Don't try to talk to me. I'm leaving."

WOMAN: The problem is that she allows the doctor to get away with his rotten language behavior. She continues to call him "doctor" in spite of his use of her first name. She lets him interrupt her, ignore her, leave her baffled, and walk out on her. And she uses a Hedge when she tries to question him. (NOTE: 'Somatization disorder' is the very latest version of the old "It's all in your head" diagnosis line.)

INTERACTION FOUR

GEORGE: George uses Blamer Mode all the time. He insists on Sight Mode, no matter what anyone else does. Even when he is repeating Phil's "I hear you" he won't give up Sight Mode. Finally, his "What IS it about you . . . " sentence is an example of a Section G attack.

PHIL: Phil is Leveling in response to George's Blaming, which is good; but he fails to match Sensory Modes. He answers George's Eye vocabulary only with Hearing Mode sequences.

BOB: He uses straight Blamer Mode, like George. He uses two Verbal Attack Patterns, and a part of a third. And he is using overt insults when he tells the others that they act like "stupid little kids."

INTERACTION FIVE

GUARD: She stays in Computer Mode through the whole interaction, even when the young man uses Leveling Mode. She keeps repeating herself, as if she can't hear what he is saying at all. And she uses a Section D attack.

MAN: If he had tried talking to this woman in Touch Mode, it might have helped, since she keeps using Touch vocabulary—but she may only be doing that because she's talking about sculptures, and *touching* sculptures. It's possible that if he had switched to Computer Mode with her she would have perceived him as more mature and trustworthy. But the only thing he did that was clearly a bad move was taking the bait in her Attack Pattern and responding directly to an attack on "young persons." He should have just said, "You're absolutely right." Or, if he was determined to defend himself (a waste of time in this case, frankly) he should have said, "The idea that young people can't be trusted is a very common one, but it's surprising to hear it from someone with training and experience like yourself."

INTERACTION SIX

WOMAN: She uses Placater Mode almost exclusively; since the young man is doing the same thing, the Placating just gets worse and worse. She goes into Blamer Mode to accuse him of trying to trick her. And when she apologizes after he objects to her accusation, she ruins the apology by using a Hedge that allows her to take it back at the same time that she's making it.

MAN: He uses Placater Mode most of the time, except for his very last line, where he switches to Blaming. He uses the crudest form of Hedge there is, when he cuts off his utterance in the middle with "OH, NEVER mind." That is a mannerism that is without exception annoying to whoever hears it.

INTERACTION SEVEN

MARY: Her first bad move comes with, "MY parents are capable of under-STANDing . . . "; the heavy stress on "my" gives the sequence the meaning, "my parents, in contrast to your parents." This is guaranteed to cause a row. When John objects, she makes things worse by Phony Leveling—pretending that she doesn't understand what he's angry about. Her final line is a vicious counterattack, structured in a way he will find hard to forgive—she humiliates him by using his own words to attack him with. And she puts him in a position where there's nothing he can say in response that won't mean a loss of face. Finally, she insists on using Sight Mode while he stays in Hearing Mode, all the way.

JOHN: His first bad move comes when he responds to the insult in Mary's "MY parents . . . " The proper response would have been to pretend he wasn't aware of the insult and to say, "Well, that's great. I'm glad it's settled." She would then have had to either accept that decision or come out into the open with her feelings. He never matches her Sensory Mode. When he falls for the trap she has set up for him, he does it in Blamer Mode; furthermore, he starts using culturally loaded vocabulary such as "snob" and "lowlife." His defense was disorganized and ineffective. And he walked right into a sucker punch when he said "I'm not the kind of wimp that . . . etc." John's language behavior is— to use a metaphor, as he ought to have done—like going out on a busy freeway and playing in the traffic.

INTERACTION EIGHT

WORKER: When Louis is told to provide the foreman with something to say to management that makes *sense*, he responds with a metaphor that is anything but unifying. He starts by comparing the closing of the parking lot to a tornado, and then goes on to compare the carpooling workers to sardines in a can. This irritates the foreman, who grabs the muddled metaphor and runs with it. Louis responds to that with a Section G Attack in Blamer Mode. This does him no good at all; the foreman uses the metaphor again to finish Louis off, and goes away laughing at him.

FOREMAN: The foreman is Leveling all the way, and he makes no mistakes. There is a very slim chance that if he had switched to Touch Mode to match Louis things might have gone a little better—but it is *awfully* slim. Chances are good that he would just have done a more effective job of wiping up the floor with Louis, given the tornado-sardine casserole his employee served up to him.

INTERACTION NINE

NIECE: No errors or bad moves.

AUNT: No errors or bad moves.

INTERACTION TEN

JEANNE: Jeanne can't be said to have made any wrong moves, because she is a person in crisis, under severe stress. In that situation she can't be expected to communicate as she would under normal conditions.

LESLIE: If Leslie is right, and Jeanne is only imagining or faking the problem, none of the things she says is going to help with that. She uses Blaming Mode, she uses Attack Patterns, and she makes open insults. If Jeanne really *is* ill, what Leslie does is not just poor communication; it is literally dangerous.

SAM: Sam does a fine job. Like Jeanne, he is under stress, because he is genuinely afraid that his sister-in-law is in real trouble. He uses straight Leveling Mode, and that is the right thing for him to do.